COPING WITH CLERGY BURNOUT

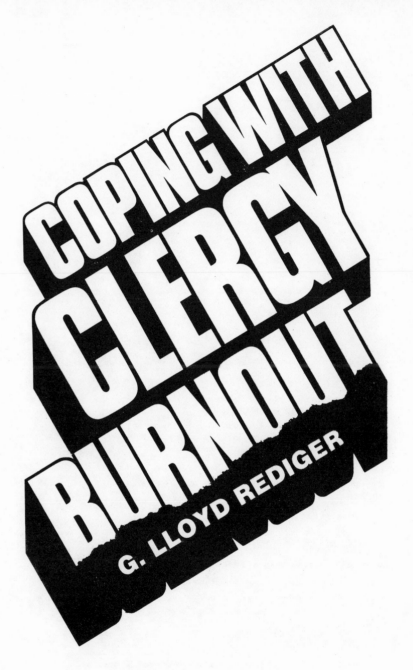

COPING WITH CLERGY BURNOUT

G. LLOYD REDIGER

Judson Press ® Valley Forge

COPING WITH CLERGY BURNOUT

Unless otherwise indicated, the Scripture quotations in this publication are
from the Revised Standard Version of the Bible copyrighted 1946, 1952 ©
1971, 1973 by the Division of Christian Education of the National Council of
the Churches of Christ in the U.S.A., and used by permission.

Also quoted in this book:
  The Holy Bible, King James Version.

Library of Congress Cataloging in Publication Data

Rediger, G. Lloyd.
  Coping with clergy burnout.

  1. Clergy—Job stress.   2. Clergy—Psychology.
3. Burn out (Psychology) I. Title.
BV4398.R42   253'.2   81-20883
ISBN 0-8170-0956-6   AACR2

To my brother, Norman, who burned himself out ministering to others

Contents

Preface

I have been encouraged to write this book by the concern of pastors, denominational executives, and congregations. They see a condition occurring in the leadership of the church which has significant negative effects on the persons involved and on the church as a whole. I pray this book will enhance understanding of the condition and encourage the development of pastoral support systems.

In dealing with any problem or opportunity, we know the value of naming it clearly and structuring our response to it in appropriate ways. This book gives the malady, the condition mentioned above, a name and presents recovery and prevention strategies. The malady has been identified in other literature regarding the helping professions. I hope the jargon use of the term "burnout" in our society does not distract us from the need to handle that condition more effectively.

The reader will note that I have used the literary device of repetition to underscore factors which I see as especially significant to this discussion.

I am indebted to the many pastors and church officials who have shared their personal experiences and insights regarding this condition. My appreciation for significant aid in editing and typing the manuscript goes to Jeanne Maruska, my highly valued administrative assistant, to Phil Rowin, an able professional and friend, and to Harold L. Twiss, who has sensitively guided this book to publication. My wife, Shirley, has made valuable suggestions from her perspective as professional management consultant. And to my father, Rev. C.

J. Rediger, goes my lifelong appreciation for his modeling of dedicated pastoring.

—GLR

Introduction

Now we have something else to worry about in the ministry—burnout. And if we worry enough, we may burn out.

This concept of burnout is relatively new in our thinking. People have burned themselves out in pursuit of an intense goal or vision for centuries, of course, and some people burn themselves out through self-neglect or self-abuse. So burnout itself is not new, but identifying the syndrome and understanding the increasing stress of modern living shows us we need to give this condition some attention.

Clergy are in a stressful vocation. We who are in the clergy need to alert ourselves to the possibility of clergy burnout and find ways not only to avoid it but to enrich our living and ministry. We can model for a hectic, stressful society the inner peace which is possible in the midst of contemporary life.

This book shares the insights gained from personal experience and many years of counseling clergy through the Office of Pastoral Services. In this book I have tried to present information about clergy burnout, give examples of it, and, finally, present a model for preventing burnout while, at the same time, enriching personal living and public ministry.

In very general terms, here are the perspectives on burnout which this book will discuss:

The Burnout Formula is: Living beyond your limits. When there is a sustained energy deficit, burnout is possible.

The Burnout Slogan is: "Try harder."

The Burnout Prescription is: The AIM model of self-care and healing. The *A* stands for awareness. The *I* stands for input. The *M* stands for management. Energy going out cannot exceed energy coming in. Try smarter, not harder.

The Converse of Burnout is: *Wholeness.* I'm referring to the biblical sense of the goal of human experience which I'll discuss later.

This book doesn't provide all the answers. It covers the subject only briefly. It is my hope that it will trigger your own creativity in handling this subject, for the best answers are the ones which come out of your own experience.

The Problem/Opportunity

1
Background and Perspective

The condition we are discussing in this book is commonly called "burnout." This is now a popular jargon word in our society. Therefore it is already loaded with misconceptions, half-truths, and mythology as well as some valuable insights.

The word burnout is descriptive of the condition. It suggests the same intense use of energy as does the verb "burn," and "out" suggests the exhaustion of resources. Both parts of the word are accurate descriptions.

In my perspective, burnout is a version of the depressive syndrome. It has many of the characteristics of depression, but it is unusual enough to require specialized attention and treatment.

I first became aware of this condition in the 1960s as I worked with community organizers, social activists, and clergy in the racial struggle. I was a local church pastor myself and intensely involved in getting black and white, church members and non-church members to understand each other and try to work together.

I was asked by my national denominational office (United Presbyerian) to come to New York and assist with the racial crisis interpretation team. Part of my work was on the streets, part was in the corporate offices of big business, and part was in local churches. I encountered highly talented and intense social activists as well as several professional community organizers. As I worked with such persons over a period of years and noticed changes in them and myself, it became evident that such highly stressful work took its toll physically, emotionally, and spiritually.

There was an awareness among professional community organizers that three years was about the maximum survival expectancy for any worker in this endeavor. By the time a person had struggled with the massive social and personal pressures of the racial struggle for that long, he or she either had divorced, had gone to some other job, had committed suicide, or had begun to exist in a land of zombie life-style markedly different from the intense and creative style the person possessed when first coming to the job.

This experience was felt by the clergy and lay social activists to some extent also. They didn't exhibit the drastic deterioration seen in the professional community organizers, for they had other jobs, interests, and relationships which tended to sustain them. However, it was apparent that, after several years of sustained involvement in the struggle, their energies and creativity, too, began to wane.

Two rules of thumb emerged for working with volunteers in racial activist circles. We began to realize that the average activist could mount an intense campaign for some racial change only about once every six months; less intense efforts could occur closer together, however. Second, the more campaigns a person had been through, the less dependable he or she became for a massive effort for social change.

The exceptions to such degeneration were the persons who had a sustaining support system (helpful family, other job, diversionary interests, and so on) or who had learned to pace themselves in their intense involvement. (They didn't stay with the battle night and day or they participated only periodically.)

When persons in the racial struggle did not take appropriate care of themselves, they began to exhibit certain characteristics. The earliest one seemed to be increasing irritability. Things which they had handled easily before began to annoy or distract them. They became whiners; instead of expressing enthusiasm for the task, they complained about not being appreciated or always having to do the unglamorous jobs or never being given enough support or resources to work with.

Another early warning sign was intensification of efforts by persons who were already going strong. They seemed to sense something was breaking down; so they tried harder to accomplish their tasks. They would eat on the run, never take time off, keep more and more erratic hours, and try to drive everyone working with them to work even harder.

There were signals of more advanced breakdown, such as sporadic effort. Persons would be high one day and low the next. They would go all out on one task and fail at another without reference to realistic priorities.

Another advanced sign was a stage of hostility and cynicism. These attitudes seemed to alternate without apparent reason. One day these persons would be ready to punish and destroy. The next they would laugh at or despair of any efforts to bring social change.

In the more advanced stages such persons often reported insomnia. Sometimes they overate. Sometimes they went long periods without eating. They would begin to miss appointments with no rational explanation. They sometimes spent long hours telling anyone who would listen of all their problems—marital, physical, family, and financial. By this time their creativity had waned. They were less able to figure out how to handle problems. They would stay with one method or project long after it was apparent to others that it wouldn't work. They were less tolerant of criticism or advice.

In the last stages before they left or collapsed, they changed drastically from what they had once been. Physical appearance deteriorated. They either would become sullen and withdrawn or would compulsively hang around anyone who wouldn't shoo them away. They developed one-track minds in which they could think of only one task or idea for hours or days. They lost all sense of humor except "gallows humor." They couldn't be playful but they could be ridiculously giddy and irresponsible. They had almost no energy for accomplishing anything. And they often developed paranoid fantasies about irrational possibilities and even about their best friends.

The burnout syndrome was not well enough known or, perhaps, the tasks seemed too urgent for the warning signals to be taken seriously. So everyone kept going on as well as he or she could, each in his or her own way, while some collapsed, some dropped out, and others paced themselves and hung in there.

After seeing this burnout process many times and having counseled pastors who are burned out, I can state more clearly what the burnout syndrome looks like in pastors.

Physically. Low energy. Weight change. Exhausted appearance. Significant change in sleep patterns. Motor difficulties such as lack of coordination, tremors, twitches. Frequent headaches and gastric upset. Loss of sexual vigor. Hypochondriacal complaints.

Emotionally. Apathy. One-track mind and loss of creativity.

Paranoid obsessions. Constant irritability. Constant worrying. Loss of humor or development of "gallows humor." Sporadic efforts to act as if everything is back to normal. Complaints of loneliness. Inability to be playful or become interested in diversionary activities. Excessive crying. Random thought patterns and inability to concentrate. Hopelessness.

Spiritually. Significant changes in moral behavior. Drastic changes in theological statements. Loss of prayer and meditational disciplines. Development of moral judgmentalism. Loss of faith in God, the church, and themselves. One-track preaching and teaching. Listless and perfunctory performance of clergy-role duties. Loss of joy and celebration in spiritual endeavors. Cynicism. A person seldom exhibits all of the above characteristics, but a combination of two or more from each of the categories usually marks the burned-out person.

It must be noted that having some of the above characteristics is also common for a person who is tired, discouraged, or bored. Just having some of these characteristics does not indicate a burned-out person. It is the depth, the pervasiveness, and the combination of these characteristics which indicate burnout, for burnout is a "more than" disorder. Burnout is more than tiredness, discouragement, or cynicism; it is the exhaustion of resources.

A person may be able to turn this newly identified syndrome into a self-fulfilling prophecy. If one worries enough about becoming burned out, one might be able to accomplish what one is worried about.

It is obvious that persons have burned themselves out for worthy and unworthy causes for centuries. But we seem to be seeing this phenomenon much more frequently in recent years.

It should also be obvious that most pastors do not burn out and that most churches are not burnout traps.

I divided the characteristics of burnout into physical, emotional, and spiritual categories for descriptive clarity, not to suggest a fragmented view of burnout. A person cannot be burned out in only one of these categories although one category may be more visibly or deeply affected. Burnout is the exhaustion of all physical, emotional, and spiritual resources.

2
Understanding Burnout

When a human condition gets as much attention as the burnout syndrome has had, it tends to attract and accumulate synonyms and ideas which become its mythology. There is some truth in all the accumulated jargon, but reality may become victim to impressions.

Words such as tension, stress, anxiety, discouragement, exhaustion, and uptightness refer to negative feelings and behavior associated with burnout. But they are not synonymous with burnout. Each of these terms has both clinical and folklore dimensions. Each symptom is experienced by normal persons as a part of normal living patterns. We may expect the normal person to recover from or handle such experiences relatively well.

The idea of burnout is threatening. It brings a fear response and fear is a very powerful human emotion. When we react out of fear, we may trigger an overreaction which has damaging effects of its own. To avoid overreaction and to gain a clear perspective on burnout, we need to ask some sensible questions, such as: "Is there really such a thing as burnout?" "If there is, how can it be clearly identified?" "Who are the potential and actual victims of burnout?" "What can be done about it if it occurs?" "What can be done to prevent it?" This book will respond to these questions.

Is there such a human condition as burnout? Can a clergyperson become burned out? After many years of parish experience and years of counseling clergy, I believe that it is a real condition and that it can afflict clergy.

Given the newness of our identification of the condition, I must also add that all the data and insights have not yet been gathered. Burnout may turn out to be an illusionary condition generated in a person's own imagination. It may be part of a different condition or disease not yet identified. It may even be a fad to be written about and forgotten when the scare is past. But in this book I am treating burnout as a real, devastating, and preventable condition.

Burnout as a human condition is a syndrome—a pattern of experiences and characteristics. It is characterized by the depth and persistence of its individual and combined factors. Being discouraged or even exhausted does not necessarily indicate that one is burned out. But such feelings are a part of the full syndrome. They can be early warning signals that burnout is starting to occur in the individual.

The pattern of experiences and characteristics we are calling burnout involves the body, mind, and spirit—the total person. (I do not intend body, mind, and spirit to be technical categories here. I simply use them to indicate the most commonly understood categories of personhood.) When a person is burned out, she or he is incapable of functioning at more than a minimal level in any of these three categories.

It is not pleasant to see or associate with a burned-out person. Such a person is capable, oftentimes, of keeping up appearances and handling minimal tasks or ones in which the person has already become competent. It doesn't take much probing or pressure, however, to expose the fragility of the person's physical, emotional, and spiritual structure. Any additional pressure will cause the person to collapse entirely or retreat quickly into a coping mode of withdrawal, apathy, or confusion. The victim often will be physically ill, accident-prone, and erratic in behavior.

The diagnostic categories I use to help identify the functioning capacities in burnout are functional, malfunctional, and dysfunctional. By functional I mean an ability to handle a task or emotion in ways commonly acceptable for the given situation. By malfunctional I mean inconsistency in handling an emotion or task in ways commonly acceptable for the given situation. And by dysfunctional I mean consistent inability to handle a task or emotion in ways commonly acceptable for the given situation.

In diagnosing burnout, therefore, I look for patterns of dysfunction. Where there is dysfunction in the majority of the crucial elements of personal and professional functioning (these elements involve body, mind, and spirit), I conclude burnout is a likely diagnosis.

There are other conditions which can produce burnout-type syndromes. Serious physical illness or organic breakdown can produce this syndrome. Traumatic events, exhaustion, or some biochemical conditions from medication, poor nutrition, or other causes, can also produce this syndrome. A careful checking of the data and the symptoms of the person will usually indicate when the assessment of burnout is appropriate.

We need to take special note of stress as a factor in contemporary life, for it is easy to mistake a consistently stressed person for a burned-out person. Often removing a person from a stressful situation produces immediate signs of recovery. This is not true for a burned-out person. Such a person usually will not function competently when removed to another situation. My experience suggests that recovery from burnout takes a long period of healing as well as removal from the stress situation. This does not mean a person cannot recover from burnout or that he or she will never again be competent. It does mean that severe burnout likely takes some kind of permanent toll on its victim.

Stress is deceptive in another way. In popular usage it is seen as a negative force, but stress is not all bad. It is something like rain. It can be valuable and nurturing. Stress is valuable in that it keeps us functioning and alert to action and danger. Just as too much rain can be devastating, so also too much stress can overwhelm our resources.

The dangerous stress factor for clergy is the intensity with which they experience a situation or handle a task. The intensity dimension of stress, not stress itself, is the culprit. Stress will always be part of the clergy experience, and it can usually be managed well. Intensity is the unnecessary part of the clergy experience and this part is what we ourselves add to typical stress.

By intensity, I mean the zealous overuse of physical, emotional, and spiritual energy. This can occur in two ways—horizontally and vertically. Horizontal intensity is that which is applied over a long period of time and to a variety of tasks and emotions. Vertical intensity is that intensity which is applied to one stress factor so that this one task or emotion is given large amounts of energy for a relatively brief time and repeated whenever this task or emotion is present.

A situation in the ministry which creates horizontal intensity in the pastor may be illustrated by a too common church game that I have called "Let's Get the Pastor."[1] In this game the pastor is subjected to a sustained and security-threatening process of resistance, harassment, and criticism which the pastor senses would end his or her career or at least force a move. He responds by pouring more effort into every job-related task.

A vertical intensity illustration is the pastor who adopts a "change agent" role[2] and pours intense effort into a change task or a social action of particular importance to him or her at every possible opportunity, usually culminating in one all-out effort to bring about a particular change.

Both horizontal and vertical intensity are frequent possibilities for clergy. The continual pressure of the role the pastor fills often seems to go on 25 hours a day, 8 days a week. The intense pressure to accomplish certain changes in a congregation or community or denomination is regularly felt by the pastor who views himself or herself as a change agent. Often there are inadequate resources for the ministry tasks. Pouring more energy into a task seems the only possible solution.[3] This is a common delusion of change agentry.

While this is not a book on clinical research, four sets of data related to our subject can help us understand the stress factor in the burnout syndrome.

The first data reference is the well-known research on stress by Hans Selye. In several books and research papers, Dr. Selye has documented the stress mechanism in human beings. Selye has said that stress is "the nonspecific response of the body to any demand made upon it."[4] When there is enough stress on a human being, an involuntary (automatic) biochemical process is triggered.

This is the well-known "flight-fight" syndrome. The first stage of this he calls "alarm." The body is preparing for all-out response to what is perceived as a threat. The second stage is "resistance." Here the body strains to resist or escape the threat, or tries to accommodate to it. If resistance does not eliminate the threat and the body cannot adapt to its presence, the third stage comes inevitably. This stage is "collapse." This theory is built upon the premise that the body has a limited energy resource. When that resource is used up, or too much of it is drained off in a short time, collapse is all that is possible.

Another significant set of data has been accumulated by Thomas

Holmes[5] and his associates. Although Dr. Holmes writes about the effects of change on human beings, his work applies also to the understanding of stress. Holmes says that any change of circumstances produces an effect upon us. Whether the change is positive or negative, it takes its toll on our energy resources.

Dr. Holmes and his associates at the University of Washington Medical School produced a list of the life-change events which typically happen to people. The events are both positive and negative. After testing the impact of each event on the psychological equilibrium of normal persons, he assigned numerical values to each item. He called these "Life Change Units." The death of a spouse, for example, turned out to have 100 LCU's of impact on the surviving spouse. A spouse going to work outside the home equals 26 LCU's. Vacation time equals 13 LCU's. Holmes says that when there is an accumulation of 200 LCU's or more in the span of a year a person becomes much more vulnerable to maladies of various kinds.

We don't need to become compulsive LCU counters like some people who anxiously count calories, but we can become aware of the significance of changes in our lives. Holmes says that any change produces stress and Selye shows us what extreme and extended stress of change does to the human body.

Abraham Maslow is another name familiar to most of us. He aids our understanding of burnout by helping us understand how our needs affect us and how the nurturing or abusing of the human need process can help us reach our potential or lapse into burnout. Maslow says there are basic human needs common to all of us even though we each experience and satisfy them in our own ways. These needs are arranged in a hierarchy. The strongest basic human need is the physical one (food, and rest, and so on). This is our survival need. The next strongest need is for security (safety). The next need is the need of belonging (our social need). Then there is the need for esteem, our affirmation need. Finally, there is our self-actualization need, our need for autonomy and for fulfilling our full potential as a person.[6]

We experience these needs as hungers. When they are not satisfied, we have a deficit feeling—a hunger that grows until it is satisfied. If the need is not met adequately for a long period of time, this deficit affects the whole person. If more than one need is not met, the danger multiplies. When the basic needs are not met adequately, the deficit in the whole person grows. When the needs are not met for a long period, the whole person begins to break down.

The fourth set of data I refer to is that accumulated in the Office of Pastoral Services.[7] Out of my ten years of service to clergy and 500 counseling files the following data emerge: Only ten pastors with whom I have worked I would identify as burned out. This obviously shows two percent as the numerical percentage for this syndrome in formal counseling at the Office of Pastoral Services.

For clarification we do need to note a skewed effect in this statistic. Persons using the service of this office are a self-selected population of clergy and clergy family members for the most part. Although a rising number are referred by denominational executives, most come voluntarily, for the office is not part of any denomination's discipline. By coming, they have identified themselves as having a problem or as persons who want some specialized aid for doing some important changing or growing in their lives and profession. Therefore we cannot conclude that two percent of all clergy are burned out. The figure may be higher or lower for the general population of clergy.

This percentage figure may seem too small and too skewed to be significant. My experience, however, says this figure indicates a serious problem. First of all, even if this figure is approximately true only for the clergy population of the state of Wisconsin,[8] it suggests that about 150 clergy are in a burned-out stage. Second, since the burnout syndrome is a state of dysfunction or serious malfunction, even 150 clergy in this condition produce a serious limitation in the local church ministry, and a high cost emotionally to themselves and their dependents, and a large financial cost to all involved. Third, because the costs to ministry, health, and church finances are often hidden by fear, guilt, and lack of understanding, the costs can go unidentified for some time.

Fourth, the church is not typically able to handle burned-out clergy very well. There is a role mystique which suggests pastors should have an infinite capacity to work and suffer and still bounce back and be solid models of Christian leadership. Until recently there has been no place for clergy to turn for help and no recourse for denominational executives except to remove a burned-out pastor or to give modest support in the hope that all would work out eventually. Fifth, the burnout condition is only the visible end result. The process of becoming burned out goes on over a period of months or years. The clergy person and his or her ministry suffer a long time before burnout becomes evident. Thus, there are very likely a significant number of clergy currently functioning at less than adequate levels of competency in ministry. Sixth, most of this devastation of personal lives and ministry that we are labeling as burnout is preventable. Therefore, the church as a whole needs to develop a realistic prevention and treatment strategy for handling burnout. Finally, the concern about burnout should not prevent clergy from continued striving for excellence. I hope this book will show clearly the difference between inappropriate, intense habits and life-styles which can lead to burnout and the sensible striving for excellence in ministry.

Another piece of data noted at the Office of Pastoral Services is that there are two levels of burnout. I have distinguished between them by calling them Burnout I and Burnout II. In this terminology, Burnout I is a state of total exhaustion. Burnout II is not only total exhaustion but also the breakdown of the physical, emotional, and spiritual organization of the person (his or her personhood).

An automobile storage battery may serve as an illustrative metaphor. A few months ago I parked my car in the lot by my office and forgot to turn off the headlights. It was early morning and very cold when I arrived. When I came out to drive home late that afternoon, I switched on the ignition and nothing happened. After I stopped screaming at myself in frustration, I used what voice I had left to phone AAA car service for aid. In a short time the man with the portable generator arrived and started my car. Then as he was preparing to leave, he said something which struck me as significant for our understanding of burnout. He said, "You know that you will need to give this battery a full recharge now if you want it to recover completely. Don't be deceived by the fact that your engine starts and your lights go on. It has been totally exhausted and needs more than the regeneration your alternator can give it in this cold weather." For me, this is an illustration of Burnout I—when a human being uses up all of his or her resources—and the prescription for its cure.

Burnout II, if we continue the car battery analogy, is illustrated by the battery not only being used up but also being damaged or beginning to disintegrate. If the battery case is cracked or the terminals damaged or the plates corroded, no amount of recharging will bring it back to its original functioning capacity. The battery must now be repaired as well as recharged.

An illustration from biblical times may also help us understand the two levels of burnout. Oil was a precious commodity for cooking and lighting. We may liken the pastor to the oil vessel which conveyed the valuable oil to all the people. During its service, the vessel undergoes a great many bruises and becomes cracked and chipped. If the vessel is finally broken, it can no longer convey the valuable oil.

In burnout, one gives away so much of oneself that one cannot fulfill ministry any longer. To persist in efforts to give more than one has to give, no matter how noble, is to set oneself up for burnout.

Burnouts I and II are both part of the same disorder. Both require healing and recovery time. Both require new living habits. However, Burnout II will likely require significant aid in the form of medication, institutional care, leave of absence, counseling, and therapy. Persons in Burnout I may be able to generate most of their own recovery, if they know how. Persons in Burnout II are often unable to recover without outside assistance.

The same symptoms listed earlier are present in both Burnout I and II. In Burnout II they are deeper, more persistent, more pervasive, and usually have been present for a longer period of time. To the professional who is counseling a burned-out person, it will soon be obvious whether the person can recover without much outside assistance or must have significant aid.

We have also learned at the Office of Pastoral Services that there are typical factors which contribute to burnout. Any one of these factors by itself is not sufficient to cause burnout, but when two or more in combination persist in the life of a person who does not nurture himself or herself adequately they help precipitate burnout.

1. The Gap Between Expectations and Reality. Persons who have high ideals and expectations and cannot adapt these to the limitations of their situations may burn out in frustration.
2. Double Binds. These are the emotional traps in life which the late Dr. Donald Jackson made famous. He pointed out the energy-draining effect when people feel trapped—as if no matter what they do, they can't win.
3. High-Intensity Living. It seems as if every commercial on TV these days urges us to consume more, to try harder, and to win at everything we do. Those who live by this philosophy are candidates for burnout unless they learn to nurture and pace themselves at a high level. Some persons can handle more intensity than others—they seem to have more energy

or are stronger in pertinent ways, but most of us do not possess endless energy.

We in the helping professions tend to have a near-fatal flaw, for these professions attract bright, sensitive, visionary people. We can always think of more to do than our human limits will allow, and we tend to think we are stronger or don't have the same needs other people have. There is also a myth among us which suggests that the truly noble or the best helpers are those who ignore their own needs and give themselves totally to others. There is some truth to this myth, for we could all be more effective in helping other persons. But to burn ourselves out in our quest to help others is not noble in most cases.

4. The Something-to-Prove Agenda. Persons who live with a chip on their shoulders or who live as if they must succeed (demonstrate their worth) at all costs often find it costs them more than they can pay. The cost may be burnout.

5. Energy Drainers. Persons who go through life with "monkeys on their backs" may burn out. These are people with habits, disorganized segments of their lives, and life-styles which drain away their physical, emotional, and spiritual energies without producing anything worthwhile. The life of the pastor who is poorly organized is generally full of these energy drainers.

6. Lack of Affirmation. When there is little or no expressed appreciation for them or their work, people come to feel that they don't matter. This drains energy.

7. Role Pressures. Pastors are the identified leaders of our society's chief moral-valuing institution. As such, they are expected to model perfection, to have all the answers to moral questions, and to make everything work out right in the church. No one, of course, can fulfill all these expectations, though most pastors surely try. They may burn out trying.

8. The Loner Life-Style. This is a common characteristic of the clergy role. It tends to put clergy in a life-style which does not include the restorative power of two-way relationships. Everyone expects clergy to care about them, but few reciprocate.

9. Life Formulas. There are formulas in each of us which are the "truths" we live by. One of the high-stress formulas some pastors live by is: "If I give my all to the church, then the

church will surely meet my needs." Since the church didn't know about this formula (or at least the pastor's version of it), it couldn't agree to it and doesn't fulfill it. This produces a feeling of frustration at the unfairness of the situation in the pastor who lives by this formula. The frustration and resultant hurt drain energy.

10. Attitude. There are some realities in life which cannot be changed. Life itself is full of ups and downs. Some people see all of this as an opportunity to create and grow. Others see it as an unfair situation and a never-ending series of problems. The circumstances will be about the same with either attitude but negativism sets people up for burnout.

3
Some Theological Considerations

A subject such as burnout can be discussed as a purely clinical subject in the light of behavioral insights and resources, but I see clergy burnout as a theological and faith issue also. I believe the insights and resources from our faith and theology are key factors in understanding and managing burnout. God has added some valuable new resources to our faith and theology in recent years so we may combine them all for a richer view of human functioning and ministry.

This is not a book on theology. However, I do wish to take this separate chapter to underscore the understandings from our theological heritage in handling stress and burnout. Faith and theological dimensions are to be found in the models for handling stress and burnout in later chapters also.

I see a direct connection between stress and sin. These words are not synonymous, however. Sin can cause stress and stress can cause sin. I am thinking of sin in the traditional theological way here—sin as a violation of God's will and as not fulfilling our potential before God.

An early biblical teaching regarding sin occurs in the Garden of Eden story. Here we see a connection between sin and stress. Humankind existed in childlike bliss before disobeying God. When Adam and Eve disobeyed God, there came a fourfold stress: alienation from God (note that Adam and Eve withdrew from God, not vice versa), alienation from each other (Adam and Eve blamed each other for initiating the disobedience), alienation from creation's natural rhythms and purposes (they misused the fruit of the tree and were exiled from the Garden), and alienation from their own inner selves (they were "afraid"—fear is the mark of alienation). There follows the story of Adam and Eve and their constant struggle marked by common human events (work, sex, family, conflict). Their salvation lay in God's remedy of sacrificing an animal and preparing its skin to cover their "nakedness." Then God showed them how to relate to the other creatures of the world and how to extract food from the ecological system.

A second theological factor relevant to a discussion of stress and burnout is the idea of change. We believe God created all things and that God is a God of purpose. It is apparent that God set in motion many interrelated cycles of change. So, if God set all these rhythms in motion, and if change occurs, then it follows that God has a purpose for change. Therefore, we need not fear change. In fact, change is a necessary component of human experience.

The change process God put in motion has a natural rhythm about it. We may assume, then, that since we are part of this rhythm system and since we are the only thinking/willful creatures (co-creators with God) in it, our task is to discover these rhythms and learn to move with them. Human beings obviously have a problem with this, however. We tend to want things to move and change in the ways we want, instead of devoting ourselves to discovering God's ways of change and growth. When our perceptions or efforts are different from God's, therefore, we are moving against God's inex-orable purposes and can expect to pay a penalty.

This suggests a third relevant theological factor—meaning. The studies of the effects of loss of meaning by Viktor Frankl[1], Abraham Maslow[2], and other behavioral scientists and theologians have only emphasized what the Scriptures have taught for centuries: Human beings without meaning and purpose will go through "random floun-derings" (Maslow's term) and the consequences in anxiety and energy loss will be heavy. We have as examples the Tower of Babel, Saul, Jonah, the church at Ephesus, and many others.

A fourth theological factor can help increase our awareness of stress and burnout. This is the concept of limits. The Garden of Eden story again is the starting place for this insight. Humankind's very first sin, according to the story, was an unwillingness to accept limits—Adam and Eve could not resist the temptation, "you will be like God ..."

We pastors are tempted to play God because we identify so closely with God. Jokes about a "Messiah Complex" remind us of this temptation. But a subtler sin against limits is the one in which we pastors act as if we do not or should not have the same limits of energy, insight, and time that we know other human beings have. We pretend we can actually take over responsibility for another person's life, marriage, family, faith, or for a congregation's growth in grace. We pretend that our marriages, families, and financial affairs will not fail like anyone else's when we don't give them appropriate attention. We pretend that we can go on and on without proper rest, change of pace, exercise, nutrition, and spiritual nurture, and that there will be no consequences. We pretend that, because we are in this noble calling called "the ministry," we somehow become free of human limits ("... you will be like God ...").

Sometimes, when the ministry calls for it, we can turn on our high intensity for extra effort for a while. But we must always pull back and have recovery time (as Jesus did when he went into the mountains to pray or went to Lazarus's house to relax), for the limits have not ceased; we have only temporarily superseded them as a baseball pitcher "reaches back for something extra" when the bases are loaded in the ninth inning.

There are the unusual times also when God may use us beyond our limits (I can do all things through Christ which strengtheneth me. Philippians 4:13, KJV; "My grace is sufficient for you ..." 2 Corinthians 12:9). However, we need to remember that such occasions are for God's purposes, not our own and are accomplished by God's power, not our own ("Not by might, nor by power, but by my Spirit, says the Lord of hosts." Zechariah 4:6).

A fifth theological factor is pertinent to this discussion. It is the primary question all human beings, including pastors, ask before every decision and action. We are often unaware that we are asking it. The question is, "What's in it for me?"

This question seems incredibly selfish at first glance. Since the church fears selfishness, we usually deny or ignore it, but the question is there just the same. The truth is that the way we respond to this question can be self-centered—when we demand that most of the benefits of life come our way most of the time. However, the question itself is not selfish. It is the survival question God built into all of us. It's what keeps us from placing our hands on a hot stove.

In overreacting to this question, we often pretend or try to ask the question, "What's in it for you?" Members of the helping professions, such as pastors, often ask this question. It is a good one as far as it goes, but because it is overreactive a rebound effect is inevitable. We tend to start meeting our own needs through manipulating others while pretending and even intending to help them. Then we begin to resemble the little Boy Scout who helps the old lady to cross the street whether she wants to go or not because he needs to do his good deed for the day. By God's grace even manipulative efforts at ministry are often helpful. How much better it would be if we learned to take time to nurture our own needs so we might minister to others' real needs, not the needs we need them to have!

Answering this primary question of life honestly and openly lets all of us deal with each other as real people, for we are all asking the same question. We then can learn the wisdom of asking ourselves the loving version of this primary question, "What's in it for us?" This is part of what I understand Jesus to mean when he commands us to love others as we love ourselves (Matthew 22:37-39), and what Peter means by "... grow in the grace ..." (2 Peter 3:18). There is so much less conflict and stress in this version of the question.

Then there is the theological factor of peace. In the Bible the desire for peace often grows out of weariness with struggle. It does feel good to rest from our labors or to have conflict resolved. This is only one kind of peace, however, and it is limited to the times when all problems and tasks have ceased, or we have collapsed, having no other option.

There is another kind of peace and rest available to the believer. This is the peace in the midst of toil and conflict (Psalm 23:5, 2 Corinthians 12:9). When we believe that we and the church belong to God and that God's purposes will be worked out, even if we can't do it all by ourselves, then we can relax and appreciate this kind of peace (Romans 8:37-39).

Yet another kind of peace is available to the follower of Jesus Christ. This is the peace of surrender. We haven't heard very much of this word surrender in recent years. Apparently it sounds too pietistic and seems to be in conflict with the powerful new cult of "human potential." (I am all for the self-awareness movement when its reference point is God's creation, not the isolated self.) However, the surrender of our ideas of how the church must operate, how believers should act, and how I should think and feel, to God's purposes brings the peace which Jesus promises to those who come unto him and learn his way (Matthew 11:28-30).

Another version of this peace is the learning of contentment—coming to terms with the givens of life (2 Corinthians 12:10, Philippians 4:11). One of the joys that comes from experience in ministry is the letting go of intense and inappropriate change agendas for self, others, and the church, when we no longer crucify ourselves on the cross of our own idealism.

Sometimes this sounds as though we are compromising our standards or forgetting our dedication or becoming lazy. It could be. However, there is a wisdom, a trust in God, which comes with experience and/or spiritual discipline. It says, for instance, of a troubled church situation, "This is God's church. It was here before I came. It will be here after I go."

As wise pastors we know that it is the Gospel and God's Spirit which produce change and ministry, not us, though we may indeed have a significant part in them. And so we learn with spiritual discipline that our response to the Great Commission of Jesus (Matthew 28:18-20) is not to change everything that is wrong with the church but to be faithful in preaching and teaching discipleship. This faithfulness is a constant characteristic of the good steward in the New Testament (Matthew 25:21; Luke 12:42, 16:10; Acts 11:23; 2 Timothy 2:2; Revelation 2:10). Being faithful drains much less energy than trying to change things ourselves.

Finally, there is the theological implication throughout Scripture of self-responsibility. I am the only person to whom God has given the responsibility for me. Others can share that responsibility, but since I am the only one who can experience, understand, and manage myself, it follows that I must accept the primary responsibility for myself before God.

I am responsible for myself first and for others second. This is not license for self-indulgence. It is a reminder of the order of my responsibility. If I nurture and manage myself modestly and responsibly, then I am capable of being an effective instrument of ministry to others. If I do not, I will be prone to meeting my powerful but suppressed needs through others. This can be a sinful manipulation of other persons that masquerades as ministry.

Now, of course, I can't meet all my needs by myself. I need other persons just as they need me. The person who recognizes his or her own needs for other persons is more likely to be open and honest in seeking nurture from them. This is better than denying such needs in oneself and then manipulating others to fulfill them. This shared process of understanding and cooperating in meeting our own and other persons' needs is becoming vitally important in a world of interdependency. There is enough for all, if all understand enough.

So the seeming nobility of self-sacrifice and denial has dangerous pitfalls. The church's teachings on sacrifice are effective only if we sacrifice our *wants*. We cannot sacrifice our *needs*, for our basic needs are part of what makes us human together. Our wants, however, are optional and are usually generated by the acquisitive and competitive programming we receive and allow ourselves to develop. These can and must be modified and even sacrificed if all creatures are to share in the resources of God's creation.

By implication, then, we may say that good theology does not honor a burned-out pastor. There are no bonus points in heaven for burning ourselves out, no matter how dedicated we pretend to be. Circumstances and sin in society may victimize some persons and pastors. This is tragic. Most burned-out pastors, however, set them- selves up for this malady. They do not seem to understand that burnout is not a mark of dedication and nobility. It is usually a demonstration that they have sinned by exceeding their limits—by playing God.

The theological and faith factors I have mentioned in this chapter are not exhaustive nor adequate for a full doctrinal approach to stress and burnout. But they indicate some of the theological guide- lines which inform my thinking and counseling. Perhaps these will stimulate you to further study to find helpful theological guidelines of your own for handling stress.

The Stress of Clergy Vocation

4
Three Case Studies

In this chapter I will present three cases of clergy burnout. They represent three different situations. The information has been altered to prevent identification of the actual persons involved but not altered enough to lose the value of the examples which each case offers us.

The first case concerns a male pastor in his mid-thirties. In both his intern year and his brief first pastorate he was an instant success. He was handsome, enthusiastic, bright, personable, and competent. He had an attractive and intelligent wife who was deeply involved in her own profession and in graduate study. She was liked by everyone but was involved in the parish very little. She managed their one child, their home, and her profession very efficiently. She was independent and enjoyed it.

This pastor had great enthusiasm for evangelism. He was a zealous caller on church visitors and new people in the community. He was continually pushing church programs which he felt would attract new members, and he talked constantly of membership and budget growth. He gave himself tirelessly to all church activities and committee meetings.

The church was located in a medium-size town. It was the second oldest church in town. The building was attractive and well-maintained but old. The church had a membership roll of over four hundred. Its members were middle-aged and older with a few young couples, a few young people, and children.

In spite of the pastor's intense evangelism efforts the church never seemed to grow although people seldom moved away. There would often be newcomers visiting, but they seldom came more than a few times. Hardly any joined the church.

It was apparent that the church did not want to grow. Several large family relationships dominated the church's committees and pro- grams. These key families represented the farm, shopkeeper, and professional segments of the community. They enjoyed their church. Most of them had grown up in the church, and they wanted it to stay the same comfortable place they had loved for so long. When visitors came, they were pleasant to them. But they managed to convey the message to visitors that they could visit and even join the church but were not welcome to assume positions of authority nor to suggest changes.

The pastor kept preaching and programming for evangelism and growth. These strong members were appreciative and accommo- dating to him. Any new programming the pastor suggested was received pleasantly. But then these members would talk it over endlessly, postpone decisions, and finally vote it down.

The pastor kept believing that they were nice people and would soon become more spiritual and enthusiastic about change. So he tried harder and harder. His anxiety and frustrations grew. His wife listened patiently when he tried to tell of his anguish, but she had her own world and was not much concerned about his.

In the seventh year of his ministry he came to our Office of Pastoral Services. He talked of his once enthusiastic but now hollow dreams of growth for his church. His body language was eloquent as he slumped deep in a chair in my office. His face and body had none of the muscle tone expected in a man his age. He sometimes stuttered when he tried to express some enthusiasm for his church. He was obsessed by his evangelism efforts.

After several visits he became more and more silent in our coun- seling sessions. There would be a blank stare into space and only sporadic comments about the church, himself, his child, and his wife. His remarks became vicious and hostile but had no energy in them. In the seventh session he began to cry and couldn't seem to stop. Several subsequent sessions were the same. He reported being unable to speak to his wife and child at home; he could only cry.

His sermons became erratic. He forgot committee meetings. He had frequent bad head colds. He couldn't sleep and he ate very little.

When I finally convinced him to go to his physician for an exam, the diagnosis was exhaustion. A delegation from his church had just gone to his denominational office and asked that he be removed as pastor. I recommended a leave of absence and therapy and he apathetically agreed. His wife's good job allowed them to stay in the home they were purchasing and to pay the bills.

As a result of his counseling and recovery, which took about a year and a half, he is now attending a university part-time, slowly preparing for the profession he had been aiming for when he had been suddenly converted and had gone off to seminary twelve years earlier. From all indications, it looks as if he will recover most of his strength and perhaps be successful in his new career.

A second case is that of a woman minister in her mid-forties. She had married as a teenager to get away from home and was divorced by her husband after about one year of marriage. There had been no children from the marriage.

She was an only child and came from a very sheltered and traditional home life. She was a bright child who had always done very well in school but had been socially inactive, choosing class plays, music, and literary pursuits over cheerleading and socializing. She and her family were always active in the church.

After working one year as a waitress and then divorcing, she went to college and did very well, majoring in philosophy and political science. She matriculated to a liberal seminary near the beginning of the social action wave in the church. There had been only three other women in the medium-size seminary her first year, but by her senior year there were thirty. She was the organizer of women's caucuses and extremely active in racial and anti-war activities. The last year of seminary she was hospitalized briefly for exhaustion, but she graduated with her class.

During seminary she had interned at a community organization office and was asked to come there full time upon graduation. Her national denominational office noted her work there and asked her to come to their headquarters and organize a new department of minority ministries. She worked very hard for two years to organize this. Then two men were moved into leadership, taking over her department. She was devastated. She brought a lawsuit against her denomination and took action in the church courts of her denomination. This struggle went on for almost three years with the denomination moving her from one meaningless job to another.

Both her civil and church judicial actions resulted in unclear decisions and she was fired from her denominational job. At this time the pastor of a large church in a metropolitan area asked her to join his staff, where there were two other pastors, both male. She took the position eagerly and immediately became active in social action and women's causes in the city. She put consistent pressure on the male pastors in her church to change what she called their sexist behavior and theology. More and more she became embroiled in conflict with her senior pastor over political issues. He responded by isolating her from the mainstream of church activities.

In her last year at this church she sought counseling and had to be hospitalized for depression. She was released three months later and returned to her position with the large church. But the situation deteriorated rapidly with intense confict between her and the church staff. She became irrational, paranoid, and exhausted. The senior pastor began to highlight her incompetent behavior and to make a case against her by saying how hard he had tried to help and to support her but could no longer do so. She was terminated.

Without a job and with little money, she sold her house and moved back to her parents' hometown where they now support her and where she is in therapy.

A third case of burnout is a male pastor in his early fifties. He had a series of small-town churches in his twenty-four years of professional ministry. He was a good preacher and marginally competent in pastoral skills. He was a bachelor for ten years of his ministry, then married a quiet middle-aged woman who treated him very kindly, like a son. They had no children.

This pastor looked like a successful businessman, with a distinguished appearance and affable manner, but he seemed consistently unable to organize himself or the churches he pastored. When he went to a new church, the people instantly liked him and expected great things but he never lived up to the expectations. Soon people showed their disappointment by criticizing him, although none of his churches had ever fired him. He seemed to work hard and faithfully, but nothing ever came of his efforts.

He grew up in a large family whose father was a warm, friendly factory worker. His mother was a quiet plodder. He was the youngest child. The three other sons and two daughters all became highly successful professionals. They moved away from home quickly but all retained warm family ties and sent money home regularly.

This pastor always had difficulty in school—academically, socially, and athletically. He was admitted into seminary on probation and probably graduated only because two older brothers had considerable financial influence at the seminary.

Since the whole family had always been very active in the church, this pastor found the church to be the safest and most comfortable place to be. However, he always felt pressure from family, peers, and congregations, who expected from his distinguished appearance, long association with the church, and his siblings' obvious successes that he should be successful, too.

He had become a covert alcoholic by the time his bishop intervened and sent him into therapy. His appearance was still that of a relatively distinguished man but inside there was little left of the man. His behavior and his rationality had slipped perceptibly, but it had happened so slowly that no one really noticed the serious difficulty this man was having.

These three cases represent different situations and personality types. There are complicating social, physical, emotional, and spiritual factors but the results are similar: a burned-out pastor with a limited future after a long period of recovery.

The first pastor mentioned is an example of Burnout I. He will likely recover because of his relative youthfulness and because he sought aid shortly after passing from the malfunctioning to the dysfunctional stage (see earlier explanation of these assessment terms). The other two pastors illustrate Burnout II. They passed from the malfunctional to the dysfunctional stage long before they received significant help. In this dysfunctional stage, not only were all energies exhausted, but personhood also began to disintegrate. These pastors will require a long recovery period.

I don't give these illustrations to frighten readers or to set up a self-judging situation. I encourage you simply to think about the patterns and the outcome, then note that pastors are human beings first and pastors second. If pastors do not learn how to nurture themselves and their interdependent relationships, they will fail in their personal lives and their ministry as surely as those to whom they preach.

5
Why
Clergy Burn Out

Most clergy do not burn out. The vast majority serve faithfully and long in their calling. But we are seeing more and more clearly that the professional ministry can be a heavily stressed vocation. Since so much of the success of ministry depends upon the local church pastor, we will be wise to take a close look at typical pressure points and provide adequate support systems.

The single most energy-draining pressure point I find among clergy is the gap between expectations and reality. Pastors are often idealistic, especially when they first come out of seminary. They are sure they can see the sins and weaknesses in the church and in individuals. They are sure that they have the answers to these problems in the Gospel and in their sincere efforts to change things.

Like banging into a stone wall or sometimes like hitting a pillow, pastors often come up against the resistance of their congregations to their wondrous ideas. Congregations often do not want to change or they want to change by themselves or they disagree as to what changes should occur. Unless pastors enjoy the taste of their own blood, they soon learn to back off, take another look at the situation, and then search more patiently for the realistic possibilities for change while continuing to minister faithfully. Of course, the problem can work the other way also: sometimes a church wants to move faster than the pastor.

I want to indicate briefly some research findings on clergy which will give us more data for understanding the typical clergyperson and clergy situation.

Margaretta Bowers[1], a New York psychiatrist and early observer of clergy in her psychiatric practice, said she found a curious and powerful characteristic in clergy. She called it "exhibitionism." She said clergy are very aware of and like the attention and power of leadership but seem to be caught in the bind of not really knowing how to lead, of loving to be authoritative while worrying about being humble.

James Dittes[2] found that a powerful factor in clergy stress is what he called "the little adult" syndrome. He suggested that clergy are overly serious and idealistic and often have been that way during much of their lives. They have difficulty playing, relaxing, compromising, and being spontaneous. They have difficulty relating to persons with more casual characteristics or who are as serious and intense as they are. It often seems that clergy were born 21 years old. They never got in enough sandpile time when growing up. (Consequently, I have a symbolic sandbox in my counseling office to remind myself and clergy not to take everything so seriously.)

Dittes also sees the pastor's conflict in the typical local church as an opportunity for pastoral faithfulness. The pressure and conflict pastors have with their churches is not unusual. The doubts about their "call" are normal. These are to be expected "in the interim"— until the Kingdom of God comes.[3]

Richard Byrd, a Minneapolis management consultant who works with clergy, says he has noted clergy are reluctant to take risks. This is certainly an indicator of their preoccupation with playing it safe. We probably all know pastors who have been removed from churches when they enraged powerful parishioners by proposing changes such persons didn't want or by not doing something they wanted done. Of course, faithfulness to the Gospel is always risky; yet to take a risk for something less important than ministry doesn't fit Jesus' suggestion that we "be wise as serpents and innocent as doves" (Matthew 10:16).

Samuel Blizzard[4] found that pastors spend a large portion of their time doing administrative work. This is work for which they had little training and from which they feel little reward. Yet they feel forced to do it because there is no one else to do it or because they are unwilling to delegate it.

Jeffrey Hadden[5] found an "identity crisis" among pastors. He saw this as a conflict between clergy and laity over authority, belief, and the mission of the church.

John Biersdorf[6] found that clergy feel frustrated because the church doesn't respond to change the way the pastor feels it should. The pastor feels caught in an organization which should be responsive to change, and yet the church keeps him or her from ministering to the changing needs in the congregation and community.

Gerald Jud[7] and his associates found many typical stresses for clergy: feelings of inadequacy, church politics, family pressures, work frustrations, and so on. When the stress of these accumulate, it seems to take only one precipitating event to push a pastor into despair or into a move out of the parish ministry.

Edgar Mills[8] has been one of the most thorough investigators of clergy stress. He finds many sources of stress—real and potential—among clergy: low salary, feelings of frustration and futility, feelings of inadequacy, spouse and family unhappiness with the church, inability to relocate, and so on.

One of Mills' most insightful findings was in the area of role conflicts.[9] He found role pressures for pastors resulting from being the identified leader of society's chief valuing institution. The pastor must deal constantly with polarities; his or her vocation is an ultimate commitment; his or her clients are his or her employers; (the pastor often feels on the periphery of society while believing ministry issues should be central; and, all three of his or her identities—personal, professional, and religious—are locked into one role: the pastor. The differing expectations at work within the pastor from parishioners, the denomination, peers, and self make it difficult for the pastor to prioritize his or her work with some hope of satisfying achievement.

Along with the information about typical pressure for clergy, we should note that there are stages in the pastor's life when the stress seems more severe and therefore is more likely to lead to burnout. Young pastors may burn themselves out when they arrive in their first or second parish and are unable to adjust the zeal of their idealism and their need to effect changes in the parish to the realities of their situation. There are at least two other typical times of deep anxiety for clergy. About ten to fifteen years into his or her career when energy is less and idealistic zeal has moderated, the pastor often feels a nagging question, "Is this the way I want to spend the rest of my professional life?" Then about ten to five years before retirement, a pastor wonders with considerable anxiety whether his or her career is all downhill now, and may continue to worry until nothing worthwhile is left.

The mid-life issues for clergy include not only the specific-role issues but also the issues which are now being identified in society as general mid-life issues. The pastor is likely to reassess his or her relationships at this time in life. This is also the time when children are leaving home to be on their own and relatives may have died; so the pastor and his or her spouse feel the need for close relationships. The half-intimacies (one-way counseling situations) of the pastorate no longer are adequate to meet the pastor's personal needs. There is a desire then to develop or initiate close relationships to fill the need for closeness to persons who appreciate the pastor as a person, not just as a pastor.

Mid-life is also a time for coming to terms with life goals and dreams. It becomes apparent in mid-life that some life goals have been met and some have not. Now realistic goals must be set for the next stage of life. If a person can't celebrate goals that were met or is overwhelmed by goals not met, a serious erosion of self-confidence and creativity takes place. Without hope, creativity, purpose, and enthusiasm, such a person is unlikely to nurture himself or herself or be active in ways which will prevent burnout and make the next stage of life worthwhile.

Retirement is a difficult time for many clergy. Pension benefits are low and the pastor often has had little opportunity to own property or accumulate savings. The role expectation that a pastor live modestly on a low salary leaves the pastor with few financial resources for retirement unless pastor and spouse both had paying jobs or learned money management skills. So the stress of impending retirement is often heavy for clergy couples, especially in our consumer-oriented society.

The dual-career issue affects clergy marriages as it does nonclergy marriages. Though clergy have tended to have dual-career marriages for a long time, due to the need for two incomes, they too, feel the confusion of gender role change (how to divide household and child-care duties). The pastor often assumes that, because he or she is so committed and busy, the spouse should accept most of the responsibility for housekeeping and child rearing. Resistance from the clergy spouse is then experienced as nonsupport.

The dual career phenomenon also raises the possibility that clergy and spouse may change and grow in differing directions. This may result in the two beginning to feel like strangers or, at least, losing the sense of closeness and shared goals they had earlier.

The sudden and rapid rise in the number of ordained women has introduced some unique stress issues. Women pastors often feel pressure to prove they are as good as men in pastoral roles, or they may see their role as doing battle with the sexism of the church as an institution. This "soldiering" attitude puts a double stress on women clergy. ("Soldiering" is simply a descriptive term to indicate the woman pastor who constantly finds, or has imposed on her, the gender battles typical of any minority moving into a new field. The theological dimension, however, adds some unique dimensions.) They not only must grow and develop as competent pastors, but they also often feel pressure to legitimize their presence in the profession in some settings.

Male pastors may feel stress with women in the ministry; they may object to ordaining women. They may want to be accepting on one level, but at a deeper level they may feel uneasy about the potential for sexual intimacy, or feel they must protect or champion women's concerns. The real crunch comes, of course, when women compete for the jobs men want or when women rise to high positions quickly because of the church's need to broaden its gender base quickly. This is too new a phenomenon for us to see how such stresses may be lessened. However, it seems obvious already that women are competent and dedicated pastors. They also are beginning to make unique role and theological contributions which should enhance ministry.

Another very new dimension of the professional ministry is the married pastor team. Husband and wife may serve in the same parish or different ones, part- or full-time. The obvious stresses lie in finding parishes willing to accept them as a team or parishes close enough for them to spend reasonable amounts of time together. Beyond the usual gender role stresses and the items mentioned above, there is little data yet on stress related to women in the ministry.[10]

Just as ordained women represent a distinctive case of clergy pressure, so clergy in specialized ministries have to cope with certain unique stresses. Military chaplains, institutional chaplains, campus pastors, pastoral counselors, professors, agency directors, and others are now establishing themselves as legitimate pastors in their areas of work in most denominations. Most wrestle with pressures which are somewhat different than those faced by the typical parish pastor.

Those in specialized ministries must cope with the stress of allegiance to their secular employer while maintaining spiritual discipline and ministry orientations. They may be expected to use their pastoral identity to manipulate clients for the benefit of a secular organization. Some must maintain multiple certifications. Some contend with interdisciplinary competitions. They must often minister to believers and non-believers alike and relate to persons in devastating conditions. They are often isolated from their denominational roots and support. Some must compete for clients, wrestle with fees and secular financing, and justify their practice to uninformed peers and public.

The multiple staff relationship is another common stress situation for clergy. Though the ideal of loving relationships seems so logical for pastors who compose a ministry team, they experience the same competitive and conflictual relationships felt wherever people try to work together. However, since there is pressure to appear compatible and dedicated, the conflicts are often camouflaged or denied, which makes them difficult to resolve and more stressful than necessary.

I mention one last stress point briefly because pastors mirror a difficult professional issue in our society. This is the stress of failure or, as it is more often experienced, the fear of failure.

Our society places such a high value on success that our value and belief systems are distorted especially when applied to vocation. Success, of course, is defined by symbols, status, and achievements unique to each profession and to personal accomplishment in general. The pastor may experience ambiguity in regard to success. If a pastor is successful in achieving status and financial accumulation, she or he will violate the Christian ideal of humility and modest consumption. If she or he is unsuccessful in these terms, the pastor (and his or her family) may feel deprived and inadequate. The Bible's teachings and clergy tradition seemed clearer and easier to carry out when clergy were unique in their role in society. Now that clergy are often seen simply as members of another profession, they must resolve this ambiguity in terms of the beliefs and values compatible to their faith and self-concept.

Our theology and faith can make us less vulnerable to the stress of failure if we accept the biblical teaching that we learn and grow through our failures. Since the church belongs to God, to view the pastor as a failure or success in the church is inappropriate, for it is not the pastor's success or failure which constitutes the church's success or failure. The pastor may more accurately judge himself or herself in reference to spiritual growth and to faithfulness to ministry which have long been standards for clergy.

6
Identifying and Caring for Burned-out Clergy

If a person needs to ask, "Am I burned out?" there is a good chance that she or he is not. However, given the mythology surrounding this subject and the fact that it has not had enough attention and clarification, it is possible to be confused in identifying a person who is actually burned out. It is also clear that the church is somewhat confused about how to care for burned-out clergy.

We do not yet have a sharply defined diagnostic category or a clear treatment or a prevention process for burned-out persons. Therefore, the assessment and care of burnout in clergy requires noting the data and making a judgment.

When a physician diagnoses "exhaustion" and a pastoral counselor, psychologist, psychiatrist, or social worker diagnoses "depression," they have a pattern of data and a professional judgment in mind. We can go through a similar process in assessing and caring for burnout in clergy. However, we in the church do not want merely to copy mental health ideology and methods. We need to add the vital spiritual dimension and understanding to our caring for each other.

In previous chapters I have indicated typical conditions and characteristics which mark a burned-out clergyperson. Let us now list these in systematic form, bearing in mind the newness of this category and the unique variations for each person.

MILIEU FOR BURNOUT

The setting for burnout is a significant part of the assessment and care process. Sometimes it is difficult to sort out the causative and the symptomatic factors in the burned-out person's milieu. Each of the following factors exists in a continuum. That is, the strength and influence of each will vary and may even be the opposite for some persons.

1. Living Quarters. When there is significant change in how a person manages personal living space, burnout is possible. For example, if his or her closet or chest of drawers was once neat and is now continually in disarray, this may be a signal of burnout.

2. Appearance. Rumpled hair and clothes which are dirty, wrinkled, or ill-chosen may indicate burnout, if worn this way inappropriately or in marked change from previous appearance. Also poor skin color, dour looks, body slouch, trembling, facial tics, slow or jerky movements may be signals.

3. Office. Disorganized, dirty, and bizarre arrangements of work space may be a sign although some creative persons maintain work space in this way.

4. Personal Affairs. Poor money management, apathetic or hostile socializing, and little or no daily planning often signal burnout.

5. Life-style. Random and decreased work patterns, withdrawn and secretive behavior, clinging desperately to one or two friends, poor relationships with spouse/family, overeating or undereating with little attention to nutritional needs, oversleeping or undersleeping, listlessness, no planning for the future, complaining or paranoid communication, or bland assurances that all is well—all may be signals of burnout.

Let us now restate the earlier listing of characteristics in terms of physical, emotional, and spiritual categories:

1. Physical. Low energy, weight change, tired appearance, sleep-pattern change, motor difficulties (tremors, stumbling, fumbling), headaches, gastric upset, loss of sexual vigor, hypochondriacal complaints.

2. Emotional. Apathy, constant worry, memory loss, one-track thinking, loss of creativity, paranoid thoughts, constant irritability, loss of humor or hostile humor, sporadic work efforts, hollow reassurances that all is well, lack of playfulness, loss of concentration, excessive crying, random thought patterns, hopelessness.

3. Spiritual. Significant changes in moral behavior, drastic changes

in theological statements, loss of prayer and meditational discipline, moral judgmentalism, loss of faith, cynicism about church and spiritual leaders, one-track preaching/teaching, listless performance of clergy-role duties, loss of joy in ministry and faith.

Let's now try to focus this assessment of burnout in yet another way. The following inventory lists burnout factors. If you wish to check yourself on the possibility of burnout, circle the number after each item which indicates your experience. Circle a number for every item.

Burnout Inventory

	Never (0)	Occasionally (1)	Average (2)	A lot (3)	Constantly (4)
1. Feel persecuted	0	1	2	3	4
2. Cry	0	1	2	3	4
3. Have low energy	0	1	2	3	4
4. Feel trapped	0	1	2	3	4
5. Worry	0	1	2	3	4
6. Have no sex interest or pleasure	0	1	2	3	4
7. Feel little excitement in anything	0	1	2	3	4
8. Feel hopeless about the future	0	1	2	3	4
9. Feel fumbling, accident-prone	0	1	2	3	4
10. Have considered suicide	0	1	2	3	4
11. Feel worthless	0	1	2	3	4
12. Worry that your mind is failing	0	1	2	3	4
13. Feel lonely/ignored	0	1	2	3	4

	Never (0)	Occasionally (1)	Average (2)	A lot (3)	Constantly (4)
14. Have temper outbursts	0	1	2	3	4
15. Can't concentrate	0	1	2	3	4
16. Feel others are watching you	0	1	2	3	4
17. Feel sloppy and careless	0	1	2	3	4
18. Blame yourself or others for anything awry	0	1	2	3	4
19. Can't pray or meditate	0	1	2	3	4
20. Feel God has abandoned you	0	1	2	3	4

21. How long have you felt bothered by the negative thinking, feelings, and behavior you have indicated? ——————weeks, —————— months, ————— years.

22. What have you told yourself is the reason for this negative pattern in your life? ——————————————————

————————————————————————————————

23. If you could change one thing about yourself, what would it be?

————————————————————————————————

24. What do you think would help you out of this negative pattern?

————————————————————————————————

25. Who would you most like to have help you? ——————————

Now add the numbers you have circled in items one through twenty. If your cumulative score for the twenty scoring items above is fifty or more, burnout is a possibility. Notice your answers to the questions with blanks (number 21-25). What do your answers tell you about your condition and how you are thinking about it? If the time span for these negative feelings is a year or more, burnout is a distinct possibility.

Clergy burnout is an attention-getter. If you find yourself going back and raising your score in the items above or extending the time-span answer or wanting an authority figure to notice your condition or talking about burnout a lot, you may be trying to get attention, seeking an excuse for poor behavior, or worrying unnecessarily about this condition. Be honest with yourself, for burnout is not a game.

The care of burned-out clergy is difficult for the church. We do not really believe clergy should ever burn out. We may tend to belittle our responsibility to care and help by saying that burnout victims are weak to begin with or that they brought it on themselves. (Even when this is true, our responsibility remains.) We are somewhat suspicious of mental health professionals (including pastoral counselors) or we tend to believe they have all the answers. In either case we do not use their resources appropriately. We tend to leave clergy (and their spouses and families) to their own resources until there is trouble. We seem to have prejudices about emotional health that keep us from dealing directly with it. We do not encourage and then support clergy to be careful in self-nurture so that burnout may be prevented, and we have few appropriate facilities and resources for caring for clergy if they are burned out.

Therefore, we need to develop a three-part program for dealing with burnout. One part should encourage and guide the self-nurture of clergy and the prevention of burnout. The second part should be an identification and intervention program for dealing with clergy burnout in its earliest stages. The third part should be honorable care and use of recovery resources.

PREVENTION

In recent years most denominations have been establishing better support systems for clergy. Sometimes this has been difficult because we feel we should not use church money for this, or we don't know how to establish a support system, or we have difficulty believing clergy actually burn out and that the church bears a responsibility for this.

Since we have seen, understood, and begun to care for burned-out clergy, the following guidelines for such care have emerged:

1. Recognize, understand, and act on the knowledge that clergy are human beings first and clergy second. This means they have normal limitations and human needs just like everyone else.

2. Actively encourage clergy to nurture and manage themselves physically, emotionally, and spiritually. This encouragement includes denominational support, modeling of such behavior at the executive level, and teaching church members at the local church level.

3. Develop a program for awareness of the early warning signals of burnout and conditions which lead to burnout.

   Danger signals can be:
   a. A pastor who works at the church too many hours with too little satisfaction.
   b. The loner-type pastor who tries to do everything by himself or herself.
   c. The pastor with no close friends and no interests outside the church.
   d. The pastor whose spouse and family make lots of trouble for him or her and give him or her little moral support.
   e. The pastor who seems to wallow in misery and is becoming hostile.
   f. The pastor who seldom takes time for spiritual nurture or continuing education.
   g. The pastor with a one-track zeal for a specific cause or program.
   h. The church that expects the pastor to do it all.
   i. The church led by a long-established power group or conflicting power groups.
   j. The church with a history of clergy "scalp hunting" (getting rid of pastors).
   k. The church which is highly judgmental and/or resistant to change.
   l. The pastor and/or church which insist there is only one way to do everything.
   m. The church and/or pastor with a strong negative pat-

tern—blaming, bickering, and so on—or with a pattern of seldom expressing affirmation for the pastor or other congregational leaders.

n. The pastor or congregation which is seldom heard from in denominational circles.

o. The pastor who exhibits two or more of the negative characteristics from each of the physical, emotional, and spiritual categories over a significant period of time.

4. Develop a distinct program for intervening, caring for, and restoring a burned-out pastor (including helping him or her move to a different location or vocation). This program needs to be made known to all clergy and congregations as an honorable and caring process. Intervention requires courage and some caring strategy and can be done effectively.

By intervention, I mean the entry of a person or group, from outside the congregation, authorized to intervene in order to evaluate and/or change the relationship between the pastor and congregation. (Intervention can obviously come for other reasons also.)

Nearly every denominational executive, pastor, and lay leader I speak with about intervention expresses some anxiety about it. Intervention certainly should not be done without appropriate reasons. But it is clear that many pastoral situations, dangerous to health and ministry, are simply allowed to deteriorate due to fear, lack of authority by qualified groups to intervene, church politics, and so on. It is likely that there are premature interventions for similar reasons.

Knowing the sensitivity of situations where intervention is needed and the variety of denominational systems of government, we can still list some guidelines for handling interventions in general:

a. Intervention can be a valuable ministry to persons and congregations and should be spoken of and explained in denominational gatherings in positive and honorable terms.

b. There will almost always be a judgment factor involved. The authoritative person(s) intervening should be prepared to make risky decisions and handle criticism, for seldom will there be approval of the decisions from everyone involved.

c. Data must be combined with judgment (good common sense plus professional insight and prayer) in doing an intervention in a dangerous pastoral relationship. Data factors include:

(1) Be aware of legal dimensions of intervention. Lawsuits are no longer an idle threat.

(2) Firsthand information is crucial. Hearsay is dangerous.

(3) There will usually be hidden agendas (motivations) involved. These should be identified and investigated when significant.

(4) Data and reports should be written so that everyone has the same information.

d. The parties involved will have different power bases and styles. This uneven power needs to be taken into account (for example, a pastor may not be completely open with a denomination executive who handles placement).

e. Confidentiality is important. It should not be used to manipulate. If the intervention is honorable, the intervention should be dealt with as openly as possible without harming parties involved.

f. The church is not a civil court. Therefore, interventions should be based upon sound theology and faith.

g. The key issue in intervention is ministry, not who wins or loses.

h. An intervention is often like major surgery. There needs to be a healing follow-up.

i. The pastor and family need and deserve special care when there is an intervention involving them, for they are usually the person(s) most deeply affected.

j. It is valuable for each denomination to develop a policy and a method for handling both preventive and post facto interventions.

5. Alert ourselves to the fact that special support or counseling resources may be needed as more women and ethnic or handicapped persons enter the ordained ministry. This is not due to their weakness in most cases, but is due, rather, to the added pressure they experience to "succeed" and the resistance they meet. Our clichés ("that's what I expected from a woman"; "black people are like that"; "we never should have

hired a handicapped person in the first place") or our facile assumptions that pastors from such groups are no different from the usual male pastor can easily keep us from developing the support systems and strategies needed to deal fairly with the variety of persons now in or entering the ordained ministry. We can have general denominational policies for handling burnout but we need to remind ourselves regularly that each burned-out pastor is a unique person who has given all she or he had to give to the church.

6. Make provision in finances, housing, therapy, and other ways to care for clergy and their spouses or families if burnout occurs. To say the church can't afford such resources is to deceive ourselves about the heavy cost of our present lack of support for burned-out or potentially burned-out clergy and their families.

Some denominations now have programs to prevent and treat clergy burnout. If you know of none, contact your denominational office or the Office of Pastoral Services of the Wisconsin Conference of Churches in Madison, Wisconsin, 53705.

A Model for Avoiding Burnout

7

The AIM Model

Stress in the pastoral situation can lead to clergy burnout when stress is handled inappropriately. The chief villain (demon?) in poorly handled stress in the pastoral setting is the intensity dimension of pastoral functioning. Hard work doesn't seem to lead to burnout but high intensity in the way clergy do their work does.

As we have seen in previous chapters, other factors can drain a pastor's energy to a dangerous level. So in being alert to danger signals and setting up a model to prevent burnout, we need a broad perspective on ministry and clergy. For the overall goal is not just to avoid burnout or to learn to manage typical clergy stress well; the goal is to enrich the clergy's ministry and to help clergy grow in grace and competence as individuals.

The primary goal of this book is to help us understand clergy burnout better and to present a model which may be useful in preventing burnout in pastors. In this last section I will present a model for prevention and then apply it to several typical issues which often generate high or sustained stress for clergy.

Models are often too general. Sometimes they do not fit a specific situation. Sometimes they seem to imply that we can solve all our problems with slogans or clever techniques. But having a model in mind can guide and trigger creativity for handling particular stress situations with specific resources.

I use several techniques in this model for simplicity and ease of remembering and applying the model. You will recognize action-inducing words, repetition, and the mnemonic device of an acronym.

I suggest that you let this model help where it can and then spin off your own model so you have a formula which works for you.

The model I am suggesting is called the AIM Model. It is a three-word guide to stress management. The letter A always stands for Aware. The letter M always stands for Manage. The middle letter is the variable word adapted to each specific problem issue.

The word AIM is itself a guideline in the model. It suggests action and intentionality. The idea of action is important because it reminds us that inertia (lack of movement) is often part of the problem. You may have noticed that sometimes we deceive ourselves into thinking we are taking action relative to a particular problem. When we are honest with ourselves, we recognize that we are actually spinning our wheels or avoiding dealing with the problem for some reason. So we remind ourselves that the AIM Model requires action relative to the problem, not wheel spinning and busy procrastination.

This does not mean we have to try harder. In fact trying harder only drains more energy and makes us more vulnerable to burnout. Therefore, our action motto is: "Don't try harder, try smarter!" Let our own awareness, data, and wise action move us past barriers we were convinced would stymie us forever.

We need to remind ourselves of another obvious factor in regard to action and to changing our action. Actions we have been taking (and the thought patterns behind them) for a long time often do not yield easily to change. We need to be wise in helping ourselves break old habits and establish new ones lest our good intentions for handling stress become nothing more than New Year's resolutions.

The second impression we have from the word AIM as an acronym is intentionality, for it obviously suggests a goal. Intentionality is a favorite jargon word in management training circles. It certainly implies goal setting and aiming for this goal rather than random actions. In the ministry we can call this random behavior "pastoring in general." It is the stressful, random ministry which is guided by the most recent phone call, the loudest protest, or the next deadline rather than by the pastoral intentionality suggested in John Biersdorf's book.[1]

The pastoral ministry is a diffuse profession. Without an organizing principle, the pastor can be like the man who jumped on his horse and rode off in all directions at once. But there is a goal in ministry. The Old Testament called it a "vision" (Proverbs 29:18, KJV). We now tend to call it our "mission." It is crucial to understand and nurture this sense of mission, for without it we flounder or burn out. With it, we have a sense of purpose and peace of mind.

The two constant words in the AIM Model are "aware" and "manage." They are of primary importance in handling each problem issue because they are the core of stress reduction.

Awareness is a crucial word for the whole human potential movement or that more recent part of it called the self-awareness movement. This movement has some traps in it, but I believe the Holy Spirit has given us a gift in the movement's emphasis on awareness. Jesus spoke several times of people who see but don't really "see," who hear but don't really "hear." This is a reminder that most of the time human beings see and hear what they want or are accustomed to seeing and hearing. They are selective in the data they allow through their mental filters. This means they can often look at the same old problem and actually see no new alternatives for handling it, or they can feel the same old stress and never let it tell them that they need to find a different way to handle the situation.

Years ago Systems Management[2] tried to teach that the starting place for change and problem solving really lies in taking time to see the situation—to notice how we are thinking about it. Try this as an awareness slogan: "Take time to think about how you are thinking about what you are thinking about!"

We all have the gift of insight—self-awareness. This is a mental faculty which sets human beings apart from the rest of creation. It is often limited by our habit patterns, by the "oughts" and "shoulds" we learned while growing up, and by lack of information. Jesus promised that he would send the Counselor (John 14:26) to guide us all into truth. However, even the Holy Spirit cannot guide us if we insist that we have all the information we need or that the way we want to handle a stress situation is the only way it can be handled.

There is a self-observer process which we can learn in order to develop our awareness. In this process we develop the ability to step outside ourselves and literally walk alongside ourselves to notice what is really happening. This usually gives a more objective view of the situation and is usually less intense than "analyzing" ourselves or worrying about ourselves. We are simply noticing our own data and letting it speak to us.

There are some questions you can ask yourself very consciously and honestly to help open up your awareness when dealing with a stressful situation. Try these in addition to any you may have found helpful already: "What is the key ministry issue here?" "Do I need more information in order to handle this situation well?" "What are the likely consequences for handling this situation in my usual way." "Would I rather have other consequences for all persons involved?" "What might happen if I took more time to think and pray about this situation?"

The other constant word in the AIM Model is "manage." Manage, of course, is a big word in business and professional circles. There is now a cult of management consultants who earn millions each year helping executives see the obvious and apply common sense to their problems. Their best contribution as consultants, it seems to me, is to come into the situation, from outside the organization, without the biases and habit patterns the organization has developed, point out the obvious facts, and help leaders apply their own creative efforts to problem solving and growth.

Do you know you can learn to do much of this for yourself? Learning to do this requires a willingness to break through the "groupthink"[3] process which has been set up in the church for handling stress and to break through your own thinking habits for handling a particular type of pressure.

Management begins with self-management. Taking charge of yourself (management) means laying aside the fantasies which keep you from doing this (or at least from doing this in some stressful areas of your life). It means giving up the fantasy that someone will come and rescue you from this stressful problem. It means rethinking the way Mom and Dad taught you always to handle a situation. Their way worked for them but it may not work for you in this situation. It means giving up the fantasy that you must please powerful people or authority figures. You will have to take them into account, but letting them dominate your thinking undercuts your ability to use the gifts God gave you for handling problems.

The word manage also means decision making, for decisions are the key to action and ministry.

You may have convinced yourself that you are a poor decision maker or that you are a good one. The truth is that everyone makes hundreds of decisions every day; yet most of us have some areas of our lives in which we find decision making difficult.

It may help you to manage better if you take some time to think these thoughts about decision making:

1. Decisions are simple. They are: yes, no, or not now; this, that,

or a combination. It is the emotional garbage (habit patterns, "oughts" and "shoulds," and believing our decisions must make everything come out right for everyone) that make decisions seem difficult.

2. No decision is irrevocable. If one doesn't work, you get to make another. Now, obviously, some decisions eliminate others but it helps to remind yourself that one decision doesn't trap you.

3. A decision must be allowed to be a decision if it is to work for you. Hassling yourself about it or remaking it keeps it from being a decision.

4. Getting in the habit of making decisions keeps you from wallowing in double binds (when it feels as if you can't win no matter what you do) and other emotional traps. There is great release from pressure when you give yourself permission to make decisions and then let them be decisions.

I don't want to suggest that all problems are solved by making quick unilateral decisions. In fact, sometimes it is best in some situations to let the persons involved work through problems over a period of time.[4] You can remind yourself, however, that refusal (or avoidance) to make a decision is in itself a decision which may set up stress, unless you have a clear purpose for your inaction and there are valuable consequences.

The middle word, and the variable word in the AIM Model is the one which starts with the letter I. It is left as a variable, dependent upon the issue. We apply a problem-specific word to each stress situation. These various key words will be presented in the following chapters as each problem is discussed.

This AIM Model applies directly to the role-specific stress for clergy. Remember that the villain in clergy stress is intensity. This intensity has two dimensions which can make it overpowering and lead to burnout. One dimension is vertical intensity—the intensity of effort and emotion applied to one situation. The other dimension is horizontal intensity—the intensity of effort and emotion extended over a long period of time. Of course, both of these dimensions can be draining our energy at the same time making clergy burnout almost certain.

In these next chapters I will apply the AIM model to several typical clergy pressure situations. And in the final chapter I will summarize a process for preventing burnout through the establishment of a support system.

8
AIM and Scheduling

To some outside observers, the clergy schedule seems like a dream come true—nothing to do all week except get ready for that one hour we work each week, the Sunday worship service. Those of us in pastoral ministry know how treacherous this open-ended, randomly defined schedule can be. Sometimes it seems as though 25 hours a day, eight days a week would not be enough time to accomplish all that needs to be done.

The clergy schedule has seasons and rhythms. When we are in tune with those rhythms, we can be comfortable. But it is easy to get out of phase with them, for they often change and flow in ways other than our biochemistry and human needs change and flow. Therefore, the key in schedule management is to take charge of our schedules and set limits or they will take charge of us and demand more than we have to give.

It should be noted that though we usually think of clergy schedule stress in terms of being overworked, there is a flip side to this problem. Some clergy are underworked and bored. This predicament usually occurs to pastors in small or inactive churches, in a multiple staff situation which is unsatisfying, or in a church whose program possibilities do not fit the pastor's talents. Sometimes this underworked pattern is due to the situation the pastor is in; sometimes it is due to his or her own inability to organize time or to develop ministry creativity.

Another dimension of this issue which is unnecessarily stressful is the clergyperson's anxiety over being a workaholic or being lazy.

The truth is that each of us has the right to choose his or her own work-style, but the choice carries consequences, good and bad. It's okay to be a workaholic when one loves one's work. (By "workaholic" I mean the person who gives lots of time and attention to work. I do not mean the intensely compulsive person.) In fact, the workaholic pastor or lay leader can be a good ministry resource. But the consequences of this work-style may be painful for those who must live and work with a workaholic. The same is true of the pastor with a more casual approach to work. This casual approach may be a good, relaxed model for our hectic society, but it may also be a tough style for others to live and work with.

In this chapter we will treat clergy schedule pressure from the perspective of the overworked pastor.

The three words of the AIM model for reducing stress in clergy scheduling are:

A stands for *aware*

I stands for *impose*

M stands for *manage*

Awareness for scheduling requires the self-observer process mentioned before. Daily and weekly habits soon engulf us if we do not have the ability to step outside ourselves and see what is really happening. This more objective process allows us to notice, for example, that we might be planning to make two hospital calls in the half hour before lunch. If we look at this expectation as a self-observer, we can note that it takes at least fifteen minutes to drive to the hospital and at least fifteen minutes for each call. The drive back to church is another fifteen minutes. So we would arrive back at church one-half hour later than we expected. At this point we realize that we will have missed most of our expected lunch hour and time to relax before the afternoon schedule begins. The resentment and frustration—energy drains from such small but cumulative errors in scheduling—can keep us intense and out of control for the week. We find ourselves consistently arriving late for meetings, having few schedule breaks for relaxation, and becoming increasingly irritable about it all.

The self-observer process usually needs some hard data to convince our habit-laden selves that change is necessary. It is valuable to take a two-week period of time in which to keep track of the actual time use in our schedules. This record will help break through our fantasies about how we are using our time, or how we feel we ought to be using our time, or will show us that we can really create more time by trying harder. There is a Task Inventory on the adjoining pages, which you may want to use as a guide to raising your consciousness of the actual time you use in each ministry activity.

The "I" word in applying the AIM Model to scheduling is "impose." We literally must impose our pastoral intentionality on our schedule or the schedule will impose its energy-draining demands on us.

The first step in imposing our intentions upon the schedule is to give ourselves permission to do so. This is not as easy or obvious as it may seem to be at first glance. Perhaps you have already noticed how reluctant you can be in some situations simply to say, "This is what I choose to do, and this is what I choose not to do." We can give ourselves all kinds of reasons (excuses?) for not using our own judgment to decide what to do and what not to do. In the back of our minds are the ancient voices of parents scolding or demanding certain behavior. Then there is the worry about what powerful Mr. Jones will say if we haven't called on his Aunt Minnie this week. A long list of these inner voices can distract us from our central purpose—being called to this church to minister, not called to please everyone. This calling means we must trust our own ability to think and to decide how to use our time and then to carry out that plan. This works if we are willing to be aware of what we are doing and honest with ourselves about it.

There are several methods by which we can focus our attention on the effective use of time. The method I find useful is the Time Bloc Method. You will find a sample Time Bloc Schedule sheet on the next page. It may be helpful.

The idea of the Time Bloc is to make your schedule visible. This should help you to be more realistic about time use and to see the pattern of your day and week. Then you will be able to lay out and adjust a schedule efficiently rather than rushing through the week with your fingers crossed hoping it will all come out right by Sunday morning.

There is no magic in the Time Bloc method by which you can manufacture more time. It simply helps you to see that there are only so many hours in each day. By managing the hours well you can accomplish ministry, be a good spouse, parent, and friend to those important to you, and nurture yourself so that there is joy in the ministry. You can come to the end of the workday with something left over, not exhausted and irritable.

Have you noticed that the actual work of the ministry really doesn't take as much time as we sometimes think it does? It is often the wallowing in indecision, procrastination, and anxiety rituals which make the tasks seem endless and the days seem long (or short!).

We've had several pastors who had trouble handling their schedules experiment with six-hour workdays. That's right—six hours! The key has been to plan ahead, lay out those schedule plans in a visible form, then go into the office (or wherever the task is to be done), do the job, and get out of there. Now this idea may sound harsh, self-centered, or "undedicated," but as a practice it can help break the "pastoring in general" pattern that leads to exhaustion, loss of joy in the ministry, and, perhaps, to burnout.

With a Time Bloc sheet in front of you, begin to fill in the 21 time blocs available for next week. The first priority is to write in the self-nurture time you have learned you need to keep your ministry rich and Gospel-centered. This includes sleep, nutrition, exercise, and study/meditation. Then fill in the time necessary to be the spouse/parent/friend to those who are dependent upon you and whom you depend upon as your support system. Then fill in the regular deadline tasks of the week. Next fill in the seasonal tasks. And finally, fill in whatever other time is available with items from your list of optional tasks. When the time blocs are filled realistically, you stop even if there seems to be more which must be done. If you want to accomplish more with your time, you must learn to make decisions, set priorities, and be efficient. Don't keep pressing more tasks into the schedule, for, when you keep adding to the work load, the time you use up is self-nurture time and time with those who need you as spouse, parent, and friend. The rule of thumb is: The more you eliminate necessary self-nurture and intimacy time, the sooner you will reach exhaustion-burnout.

The third word in the AIM model applied to scheduling is "manage." The word manage is preferable to the word "control." Control is a fantasy word that implies rigidly manipulating self, others, and situations that we often do not have the power to do. The word manage is a more relaxed word emphasizing the thoughtful directing of resources rather than the compulsive and intense manipulation implied in the word control.

Three factors that can add to your effectiveness in management are "prime time," "monkeys," and "pacing." By prime time I mean awareness of the biorhythms of your day. Everyone has high and low energy rhythms each day. If you become aware of your prime time (high-energy time), you can schedule tasks which need high energy for your prime time and fill secondary time (low-energy time) with less demanding tasks. Violating your own energy rhythms drains energy unnecessarily. Planning around your energy levels doesn't mean that you are pampering yourself. It simply means that you are honoring the way God created you instead of implying that God made a mistake.

Another helpful factor in managing a schedule is watching for the "monkeys" on your back. This simply means noticing when a task is worrying you or getting the procrastination treatment (an unpleasant letter that needs to be written; a person you need to call on, a pile of papers on your desk, and so on). When you notice a task is bugging you like this, it has become a monkey on your back and needs immediate attention. Make an exact decision about when you will take care of this task or do the task right now. You may want to have a "monkey file" in which you keep notes about how you handle what bugs you, such as the rule "Handle a piece of paper (letter, report, etc.) only once." The secret here is to notice when a monkey is on your back. Unless you want to specialize in the care and feeding of monkeys, these uncomfortable tasks can drain energy excessively.

A third management factor which may be helpful is the idea of pacing. Athletes are often taught how to pace themselves in sports. They learn not to pour more energy and attention into any phase of the game than is necessary but to save the burst of energy for crucial times. So in ministry we can break up our long work spans (daily, weekly, yearly) into smaller parts and take time for a brief diversion (exercise, daydream, catnap, and so on) even when we don't feel we need it or don't have time for it. In the long run this allows conservation of energy and gives us effectiveness longer. It's somewhat like using a car battery. We learn that short efforts to start the car engine are better than long cranking efforts which wear the battery down quickly to the no-energy level.

When we have used our awareness to gather data on our scheduling and then have laid out our daily and weekly schedule with intentionality imposed on the time available, we are ready for managing. Of course, the managing has already begun in the previous two steps.

As indicated earlier, the key to managing is decision making. The effective manager develops perspective (awareness-vision), gathers data (realistic-vision), and then gives himself or herself permission to put the resources and needs together with the priorities that his or her training, experience, and spiritual insight have chosen. There is no way the pastor as manager will please everyone, make everything turn into perfect Christianity, or fulfill all his or her personal dreams. But spiritual faithfulness and simple decision making can make ministry turn out well much of the time. The rest is up to God, as it always has been and always will be.

It is important to note that when the pastor takes the time to do a study of his or her time use and lays out a visible schedule, he provides the congregation (and spouse/family) with a valuable tool with which to understand the pastoral schedule. They are less likely to criticize or interrupt at inappropriate times when they can see the pastor's schedule.

Task Inventory

This form surveys your ministry or other tasks and quantifies three key factors to give you a quantified measure for specific tasks and a total for all tasks. It can be used to compare various tasks or total tasks within your own life or profession and in comparison with other persons.

Seven (an arbitrary number) major categories are provided for with space for you to name your own specific tasks in each category. You may wish instead to indicate the same tasks as other persons with whom you are making a comparison. The major task categories depend upon what you intend to inventory.

The "Responsibility Level" column indicates whether you have primary, secondary, or shared (between more than two persons) responsibility for a task. Indicate number 1 for primary, 2 for secondary, and 3 for shared responsibility in this column. Zero, of course, will indicate no responsibility.

The "Time Use" column indicates the usual amount of time you spend on this task in the time span you wish to measure. Indicate with a number from 1 to 10 the percentage of time you spend on this task. For example: if you spend 5 hours of a 50-hour week on this task, place a 10 in this column. Less than 5 in a 50-hour week would be indicated by a figure less than 10. (You may wish to chart a week or month of time use on a separate pie-shaped chart to visualize the percent of your time used in each task. See the Time Use Chart.) You will need to keep a daily log of your time use for the time you wish to study.

The "Satisfaction Level" column indicates the satisfaction you experience in performing each task. Use the numbers 1 through 5, with 1 being low and 5 being high, to indicate your level of satisfaction.

Add your scores across the page and then add each column for the grand totals. High totals indicate low pressure for the task, and low totals equal high pressure for a task.

There are many other possibilities for the interpretation of the numbers you generate in this chart. For example: multiply the satisfaction number and the responsibility level of one task to get a satisfaction quotient (impact of pleasure from doing something you enjoy and being responsible/expected to do it), and then compare this quotient with that for your other tasks. It will probably not be helpful, however, to over-interpret these statistics or manipulate them unless you are good at this or do it with a competent professional.

Task Inventory Sheet

TASK	Respon-sibility Level	Time Use	Satis-faction Level	Total
1. _____				
_____				
_____				
_____				
2. _____				
_____				
_____				
3. _____				
_____				
_____				
_____				
4. _____				
_____				

Task Inventory Sheet

TASK	Respon-sibility Level	Time Use	Satis-faction Level	Total
5. _____				
6. _____				
7. Other _____				

Your name _____   Date _____

Time Use Chart

In order to get a clearer picture of your use of time in ministry or other tasks, you may want to use this pie-shaped chart.

Decide what time period you wish to chart (one week, two weeks, one month, etc.). Keep a detailed record of the amount of time you spend on each of the major task categories. Compute these time figures into the percentage of total time used in all ministry for the time period you are charting. Divide the circle ("pie shape") according to these percentages for a visual representation of your time use.

An example is shown for ministry tasks. Other tasks can be indicated by the same method.

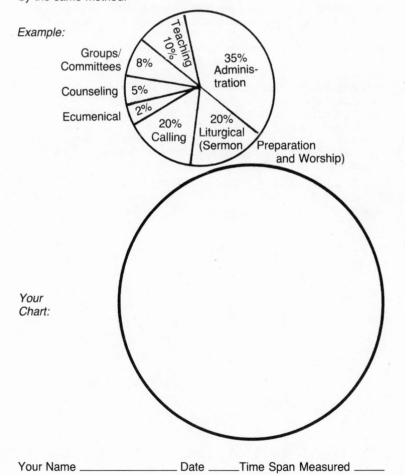

Example:

Groups/Committees 8%

Counseling 5%

Ecumenical 2%

Teaching 10%

35% Administration

20% Calling

20% Liturgical (Sermon Preparation and Worship)

Your Chart:

Your Name _____ Date _____ Time Span Measured _____

Time-Bloc Schedule
Indicator

Two of the pastor's biggest problems in organizing a schedule are "pastoring in general" (trying to do everything, and moving through activities randomly) and unrealistic expectations concerning time use (his or her own expectations and those of parishioners). This form may help in the handling of time.

Use this form to organize your schedule and to handle your time limits realistically. Decide how many time blocs you can devote to the church. Fill in those blocs with scheduled or priority functions and activities. Fill in the other time blocs with your personal, family, and marital activities. Be as faithful to yourself and family as to your work. Notice that realistic filling in of the time blocs forces you to decide about activities, not simply be overwhelmed by them. This chart also can help you communicate your time use to others and help them face realistic limits. Avoid carrying work activities into the time blocs set aside for family, marriage, and yourself.

Each indicated time bloc for morning, afternoon, and evening represents four hours. It is recommended that you stay with this format for clarity. Obviously, you may adjust these time periods to meet your needs, but stay with the plan and let it work for you.

At the bottom of this page, list secondary priority activities so you are prepared to make good use of your time if planned activities fail to materialize.

SECONDARY ACTIVITIES:

Time-Bloc Schedule Indicator   Date _____

	MONDAY	TUESDAY	WEDNESDAY	THURSDAY	FRIDAY	SATURDAY	SUNDAY
OPEN							
MORNING							
LUNCH							
AFTERNOON							

SUPPER

EVENING		
OPEN		
SLEEP		

REMINDERS, OR TOTALS OF TIME USE: _____

9
AIM and Intimacy

Intimacy is a difficult subject in our society but even more so in the church. We confuse the word intimacy with sex and, of course, we all know that the church panics at the idea of sex. Intimacy may include sex where appropriate but intimacy is far more than sex. It is the openness, closeness, and sharing of two or more people who recognize their needs, choose to be vulnerable to each other, and then accept the responsibility to support each other in realistic ways. Intimacy is closeness by agreement.

We all need other persons. No one is able to meet all his or her needs alone. Furthermore, our commitments and roles place us in dependent relationships where intimacy needs are a high priority. Since everyone's intimacy and dependency needs are somewhat different, they require that persons choosing to be dependent upon each other and share intimacy take lots of time for continually learning of each other's needs and joys and for developing the skill of negotiation where needs and resources do not fit easily.

We teach our children and young people all kinds of skills to help them be successful in life. We teach them how to clean and nurture themselves, how to drive a car, how to be plumbers, farmers, teachers, and so on. But we seem too uncertain and frightened to teach them the one skill on which so much of their happiness and competence will depend in life—how to handle intimate relationships.

In the church we tend to handle our fear of intimacy by teaching our young people vaguely about "loving," "caring," and "responsibility." Though this may sound very spiritual, it really doesn't help them understand the nitty-gritty of everyday intimacy. So youth grow up, even in the church, without really knowing how to relate to a spouse, family, or close friends.

We assume intimacy skills will be automatic in marriage, family, and close friendships (or in the church). Actually the opposite is true. The normal human tendencies are for people to be self-centered and expect other people to be the way they need them to be. This means that people require a careful learning process in intimacy if intimacy is to produce the support, happiness, and ministry we all hope for. The church should be leading the way in teaching intimacy, not lagging behind or wasting its energy criticizing what other institutions are trying to do to help with this problem in society.

The pastor is in a vulnerable position regarding intimacy in society and in the church. If the pastor takes too active a role in teaching intimacy, then criticism and rumors may result. If not active enough, then intimacy is not handled well in the church.

In many years of counseling clergy, I find intimacy is consistently an energy-draining issue. Therefore, we apply the AIM model to it.

The three words in the AIM model as applied to intimacy are:

A stands for *aware*

I stands for *invest*

M stands for *manage*

Contrary to what some people think, having sexual affairs or counseling persons of the opposite sex are not the big hazards or energy drains of the pastoral ministry. Such counseling can be a problem, and affairs represent potential disasters. But most pastors manage the counseling rather well, and avoid the affairs.

The two biggest stress factors in intimacy for pastors are "half-intimacies" and "dependent intimacies." By half-intimacies I mean the way a pastor and parishioner ordinarily relate to each other. The parishioner usually feels free to disclose very personal feelings and needs to the pastor but the pastor seldom feels free to do the same with the parishioner. This results in a one-way intimacy or half-intimacy that is only half satisfying. Often pastors speak of relating to people endlessly yet still feeling lonely. Pastors give but do not receive much in return in terms of intimacy. Therefore, there is a kind of quiet, deficit feeling that grows in which pastors wonder when it's their turn to get their needs met, who cares about their feelings, or what's wrong with them for feeling this way.

This deficit may be carried over to the marriage and family situation and may contribute to the other stress factor for clergy, the "dependent intimacies." By this term I mean the marital, family, and close-friend relationships upon which clergy are highly dependent for moral support and where the persons involved are highly dependent upon the clergyperson.

The complaint from clergy spouses and family members which I hear most often is, "she/he seems to have time for everyone else but me (us)." It seems that all it takes for a parishioner to get the pastor's attention is a phone call, a relayed message, or a committee meeting while spouse and family must rage or plead for time, or make do without the pastor. Even when the pastor is present with them, his or her mind seems to be on church activities or he or she will be exhausted and want to be quiet or want to have family members do his or her bidding without question. Family members come to feel that they matter to the pastor only when he or she needs them for something or feels like relating to them.

Now if we put the half-intimacy feelings of the pastor together with the dependent intimacy feelings of spouse, family, and close friends, we get the effect of ships passing in the night. Each wants to make contact, but the darkness (the clergy role expectations) and the fact that the ships are heading in the opposite direction (the pastor, and spouse and family searching for ways to get personal needs met rather than trying to understand each others') almost guarantee that any intimate contact will be brief and the distance between the persons will increase. If we stay with the ships-passing-in-the-night analogy, we can see the obvious solutions. The ships can pause regularly when they pass and extend the time together. They can each go their separate ways and agree to meet and spend time together in port. Or they can alter their courses and periodically sail side by side.

There are more issues we could deal with in clergy intimacy but let's apply the AIM model to the ones I've mentioned.

The awareness process opens us to the wider perspective of each person's feelings and needs. One awareness need is the fact that intimate partners are often of different sex and/or age. This means the partners will have very different feelings and needs. Even if the participants are the same sex and same age, they have different backgrounds, talents, and biochemistry. It would be folly to project our limited experience and awareness on the other person. It would result in "mindreading"—making assumptions about each other, projecting one's needs on the other. Mindreading often gives the participants the feeling that one person doesn't really care about the other or at least hasn't taken the time to understand the other's real feelings. So we end up in pseudo-intimate relationships with fantasy spouses or fantasy family members, not because each person doesn't really exist but because not enough time is spent together sorting out the assumptions from the realities.

Awareness helps us begin to notice how really different and alike two people are, and to realize how important it is to spend time together talking and listening and comparing feelings and negotiating differences. We often assume that, because we've been married a long time or once talked a lot to each other or are members of the same family, we will automatically understand each other. This is untrue, for persons, needs, and situations change. That is why there is no substitute for spending time together when we expect to enjoy intimacy with another. We also learn, of course, that there must be a sensitive rhythm combining togetherness and privacy; both are important in a relationship.

Awareness then reduces stress when we understand each other's needs and differences and take time together for building and nurturing intimacy. Without this, the pastor's marriage, family, and close relationships will fail as surely as anyone else's will.

The second word in the AIM model applied to intimacy is "invest." As you will notice, our attention to this word builds upon what was covered under "awareness" because the key point about it is the need to spend time together.

I want to emphasize two particularly important implications in the word "invest." These are learning each other's "language of love"[1] and practicing "The Love Principle."

You may have noticed how often attempts to communicate love and caring to another person do not convey the message intended nor produce the desired effects. An example would be the man who brings a special box of candy to his wife on her birthday to say, "I love you." When she unwraps the gift and sees what it is, she throws it on the floor and stalks out of the room saying, "You don't really love me at all!" The man hadn't bothered to find out that his wife had been trying to diet and was expecting a different gift. The woman didn't bother to communicate her situation and expectations to her husband. The result? No love was communicated or felt—and won't be unless this couple now takes the time to talk this over, discover the realities of the situation, and then learn to say I love you to each other in ways which really say "I love you," in language (and behavior) both can accept as love.

A particularly sensitive area of missed communication with love is in sexual intimacy. There is a difference in how and when men and women need expressions of love. For men, the more anxious they are, the more attractive orgasm seems as an affirmation of sexual worth and as a release of tension. For women, intercourse is often unattractive unless all responsibilities are taken care of and they are relaxed, and they are assured of their value as persons rather than as sex objects. Under pressure, then, men and women are often moving in opposite directions in terms of what they find satisfying in sexual intimacy. This means both need to understand the legitimacy of these seemingly opposite needs. Both need to learn to give "love gifts"—the man sometimes expressing physical affection without intercourse and the woman sometimes sharing intercourse when she only wants to be touched and held.

The intimate physical sharing between spouses, family members, and even close friends can be very satisfying when sexual intimacies are kept in their appropriate place and each person's needs are honored.

"The Love Principle" is a simple but powerful teaching of Jesus in the Sermon on the Mount. He said, "Where your treasure is, there will your heart be also" (Matthew 6:21). There is no way that I won't love a person in whom I am investing (time, commitment, understanding, compliments, support, sex, money, and so on), and it is unlikely that I will continue to love a person in whom I no longer invest.

For the busy pastor who knows that half-intimacies are not enough and that dependent intimacies require the honoring of each participant's needs, the daily and weekly schedule will have to be managed to make possible the undergirding of a personal support system which will keep the deficit feelings and inequities of relationships from becoming dangerous drains on the energy system. I will discuss this support system in the final chapter.

10
AIM and
Church Politics

Church politics is another one of those subjects we handle with ambivalence. On the one hand we want to deny that politics are important in the church. On the other hand we all know that politics are important. On the one hand we tend to think politics are all bad, while on the other hand we know that it takes politics for the church to function as an organization. This ambivalence about politics makes it difficult to deal realistically with the organizational dimension of the church. We then use a great deal of energy in anger, conflict, denial, and manipulation, and this unnecessary intensity in coping with politics can contribute to burnout. (By "church politics" I mean the actual mixture of words and actions an organized religious body uses to pursue its organized existence.)

In applying the AIM model to church politics the key words are:

A stands for *aware*

I stands for *imprint*

M stands for *manage*

Awareness in dealing with the stress of church politics begins with acceptance of politics as a fact in the local church, the denomination, and the ecumenical church. We cause ourselves great pain when we believe the church operates on perfect Christian love, and we catch ourselves in an emotional bind when we pretend church politics is good when it works for us and bad when it doesn't.

James Gustafson[1] warned us years ago of the danger in idealizing the church. He showed that no matter how we idealize it, the church will continue to be a social institution like any other social institution.

That is, it will have a power structure, internal conflicts, and traditions. However, in the case of the church we believe that somewhere in it is the "body of Christ" acting as a spiritual leaven on the church and on society. This faith is what keeps many of us in the church. It helps us understand Jesus' suggestions that the kingdom of God is not yet come and that the kingdom is within us, not necessarily in our organizations.

It may also be reassuring to add to our awareness that God can work through our politics as surely as through our love. We can remind ourselves that people involved in administrative decisions are sensitive to the human pain such decisions sometimes cause. Decision makers simply do the best they can, for they are caught in the system, too.

In its noblest forms, church politics can produce great ministries. Dedicated leaders, caring helpers, sincere ministry strategy, and sacrificial giving of resources continue to spread the message of salvation and bring assistance to all parts of the world.

Our awareness of church politics means not only acceptance but also understanding. If the church is run in large measure by politics, then it follows that those who will be most successful in leading the church will be those who accept and understand the fact of church politics. Learning how the system works has always been one of the maturing tasks of the pastor. Pastors may not like all of the political dimension—much of it may be bad, even sinful—but they can reduce their stress by accepting and understanding church politics even if they choose to fight parts of it or are hurt by it.

The second word is "imprint." It reminds us of a simple fact about political systems. We need to imprint, make an impression on, the political system if we expect it to take us seriously or to respond positively to our leadership. This happens in three ways. One is by gaining power within the system. Another is by developing power within ourselves outside the system so that the system must come to terms with us or need our resources. The third is the sometimes mysterious and miraculous intervention we can only explain as the Holy Spirit working in our midst ("charisma").

The third word is "manage" again. Here the task is decision making relevant to a political system. Our first level of decision making lies in deciding whether or not to accept and participate in church politics. The second level lies in learning and participating in the system if we accept it or learning to live and minister outside it if we choose not to participate. The third level lies in trying to blend our understanding of Christian love with the sometimes harsh realities of church politics. And the fourth level of decision making lies in helping our spouse, family members, and parishioners understand and work with church politics and the good and bad consequences of political activity.

As leaders in the church we have the right and responsibility to make decisions regarding church politics at all four levels. As always, our decisions will have consequences. By the decisions we make, we decide what consequences we live with.

The negative consequences of church politics can be harsh and unfair but Jesus never promised us that ministry or the church would be fair. Look at what the church of his day did to him! This is not to justify the pain and sin in church politics but to remind us that our mission as pastors is to make disciples and to be faithful stewards. People who lose track of this mission often set themselves up for extra pain by imagining that the church should make them comfortable. Church politics don't operate this way most of the time—nor are God's purposes designed for our comfort.

I listen to stories of the injustice and pain caused by church politics nearly every day. Sometimes I cry and rage at the system with my counselees, for the pain and sin are obvious. But we have another management task as applied to church politics: to preside at our own healing when we've been wounded by politics and to assist in the healing of other victims. Sometimes we simply must fight to change the system. Our choice to fight should relate to our spiritual imperative rather than to our personal wishes.

Another management task in dealing with church politics is to bring to it consistently our best wisdom and spiritual nurture. This requires patience at times and prophetic challenge at other times. Perhaps, most important of all, the task requires treating each other as children of God rather than as objects of our political convictions.

This chapter has dealt briefly with a difficult subject in the church. It may have sounded crass or compromising to some. I have simply shared my experience and beliefs. I invite you to reduce your stress with me by bringing your version of the AIM model in politics to bear on the church so we may all share in the progress God can bring us even in the midst of our politics.

11
AIM and Volunteers

Another of the consistent stress issues in the church is the fact that the pastor is usually a paid professional while church members (and the pastor's spouse and family members) are volunteers.

Church members are part of the church voluntarily, for the most part. They participate in the church and its responsibilities and activities by choice. The pastor is in the church by calling, of course, but she or he is also there by professional design and is being paid for this work.

From a hierarchical perspective, above the pastor is a structured and paid denominational organization. Below the pastor all are volunteers. Thus the pastor is caught in an organizational crunch. While policy and organizational discipline are tight above him or her and reinforced by the power of a paycheck, below him or her the action is all voluntary with little disciplinary clout and usually no paychecks involved. Therefore, while the hierarchical system can put a great deal of organizational pressure on the pastor, the pastor must usually find altogether different ways to motivate and direct the behavior of those below him or her.

We have all recognized this problem. Over the centuries various church organizational forms have evolved to handle it. Though the situation produces stress, it also produces ministry. Since none of us has the power to change it completely and since God apparently chooses to work through it, we must come to terms with this arrangement as a given. This, of course, doesn't mean we have to like all of it or submit to its evils without question. It does mean, as in the case of church politics, that we can lessen our stress by coming to terms with this system and learning to minister faithfully within it.

The three words in the AIM model as applied to volunteers are:

A stands for *aware*

I stands for *interpret*

M stands for *manage*

The A stands for "awareness" again, for awareness of what really happens when a paid leader tries to lead volunteers is crucial. Pastors often have high ideals for the church and their ministry; they can't understand why others don't see the matter as clearly as they do. This vision of what God expects from the church is important, but we must also be aware that God speaks to and through lay persons as well as to and through pastors. We remind ourselves as pastors, too, that, even when dedicated and willing, lay members of the church are volunteers not professionals. This means they will often have limited knowledge and perspective to bring to their ministry tasks. It means they will have limited time, energy, and money to invest since most of their efforts are used in other legitimate tasks and responsibilities.

In this awareness we remind ourselves of, and work to improve our own, strengths and weaknesses as well as the strengths and weaknesses in the hierarchy above us. We teach, delegate, and support the volunteers we are to lead.

There is a special area of awareness here for the pastor in understanding his or her spouse and family's involvement in the church. Spouse and family sometimes resent the "fishbowl" dimension of clergy life. They often resent what happens to the pastor (and therefore to them) in the crunch from the church hierarchy above and from the voluntary participants below. In their reactions, they may not handle their participation in the church with ease or according to the pastor's wishes.

These situations are changing somewhat in recent years as denominational discipline lessens and church members seem to accept more freedom of participation and behavior on the part of the clergy spouse and family members. But the awareness burden lies most heavily on the pastor in this situation. His or her patience and understanding are crucial, for his or her spouse and family members are volunteers in the church also, unless we believe that when the congregation employs a pastor, they employ the whole family as well.

The "I" word here is "interpret." A crucial function for the pastor in working with volunteers is interpretation. Again there are several levels of this important function. One level is to interpret the views and needs of the volunteers to the hierarchical structure above. Another is to interpret various groups to each other within the local church. Sometimes this activity is called conflict resolution and the process works best when there is clear communication and interpretation between different groups in the congregation before a conflict situation. Much of this process depends upon the pastor.

Another level of interpretation is to help church members understand the needs for ministry within the church and in the world around it. The means of response to these needs are often related to the denomination with which the congregation is affiliated and this relationship requires more interpretation. Many members are concerned and want to participate, but the pastor is usually more aware and informed about these needs than other church members.

Yet another level lies in the pastor's own spiritual formation and development. It is important that the pastor spend time in study, prayer, and reflection so that his or her interpretation of the Gospel and ministry is as clearly informed by God's Spirit as possible. We can all see instances in other pastors of distortion in interpretation due to biases, lack of information, and lack of skill. However, our primary task before God is to see these distortions within ourselves and correct them with God's help and a little help from our friends (and enemies!).

The management part of dealing with the stress of leading volunteers lies again primarily in decision making, not only in our decision making but also in our helping volunteers to make good decisions. This often requires us to spend time teaching and exposing volunteers to information and relevant experiences.

A great temptation when leading volunteers is simply to do the work ourselves. To train volunteers in the ministry seems too time-consuming and hopeless; yet this is the model Jesus gave us in the early church. He spent great portions of his time teaching and training disciples. He had the wisdom to see this as a priority and the grace to live with imperfect results. He knew that people will work more responsibly for a ministry in which they share than for one in which they feel they are carrying out someone's orders.

In leading volunteers there are some management guidelines which may be helpful. One is: no surprises! Keeping volunteers informed reassures them that they won't be caught off guard or embarrassed. Another guideline is: no failures. Although this is obviously idealistic, one management task is to help volunteers succeed so that they grow in enthusiasm and confidence. We can aid this growth by removing some of the fear of failure. When there is failure, we can help to keep it from turning into that devastating emotion called shame. Failure can be a great learning experience and it is likely to happen to everyone sometime. Therefore, effort spent turning failure into a learning experience rather than a shameful experience is important for ministry.

Pastors have a valuable resource in the theological formulas of the Bible when managing volunteers. For example, there is the forgiveness formula for handling hurt in the organization. Its steps are: hearing the Gospel, confessing our sin, receiving and giving forgiveness, making restitution where possible, and pronouncing absolution ("It is finished, I won't carry it as a grudge."). There is the conflict resolution formula in Acts 15. There is the exorcism formula in Mark 9 where Jesus taught how to get rid of the demonic problems in our midst. There is the love formula for interpersonal relations in 1 Corinthians 13. Many others are available to us for the sake of ministry.

Since the pastor must manage volunteers without the clout of a paycheck, she or he must learn the skills of managing with other incentives. This often means that the pastor must take continuing education courses to learn other management methods, for most pastors receive very little of this kind of training in seminary. The pastor also must learn to lead by modeling as Jesus and Paul modeled. Again, this does not mean that the pastor does all the work. It means that she or he shows volunteers how and then lets them do it.

Finally, a great management tool with volunteers and one which requires great patience is the power of invitation. The apostle Paul gave us a great example of this in the last words of the twelfth chapter of 1 Corinthians. After discussing spiritual gifts and their conflicts and uses in the church he said, "... and I will show you a still more excellent way" (1 Corinthians 12:31). Then he proceeded to write the great instruction on Christian love. Though it requires great patience, humility, and trust in God's handling of the church, pastors do well to stand before their parishioners continually saying, "Behold, I show you a more excellent way!"

The Appendix discusses the power of invitation in more detail and provides a chart for understanding the agendas from which people operate.

The management of volunteers is one of the most difficult and stressful tasks pastors have. Perhaps the AIM model and your own insights will lessen the stress of this task for you.

12
AIM and Change Agentry

In recent years seminary training and the world situation have emphasized a relatively new role for pastors. This is the role of Change Agent. This role is not totally new, for church leaders have often led the way in social change. In recent years the role has become more focused and intentional. In fact, some pastors have taken the role as their primary identity and task.

No role model or pastoral effort is more likely to generate great stress. Its pursuit can clearly lead to clergy burnout. I am not suggesting that pastors can't be change agents or that change isn't needed. I am reporting from years of counseling clergy that the Change Agent model of ministry has serious dangers and carries with it a high level of stress.

There are clear models of change agentry in both the Old and the New Testaments. However, it seems to me that we have distorted the work of the prophet and the evangelist when we try to use these models as the basis for the primary role of the pastor being that of a social-activist change agent.

God knows the church and the world are crying out in the pain of social injustice. The need for change is obvious and urgent and the role of pastor is to participate in change whenever possible. However, the primary role of the pastor is found in the New Testament model of Jesus and his Great Commission to all followers.

Jesus didn't function primarily as a change agent, but he spent much time teaching and modeling the Gospel. His commission to his followers did not say anything about changing the world, but he did mandate us to teach and make disciples. We have very clear models for doing what he taught and mandated in the example and the models of early church leaders also.

Again I emphasize that being a change agent is a needed and valuable function of pastoral ministry but it is not the primary function. If we try to make it so, we are in trouble two ways. First, we often impatiently grab the responsibility for changing things from the Holy Spirit simply because the situation fits our style or we are outraged or we love the feeling of the power to punish, induce guilt, or control people. The right to change people belongs only to God and the only legitimate power for change is exercised through disciplined followers of Jesus who take their direction from the Holy Spirit in their midst. It is the Gospel and the Holy Spirit which have the right and power to change people. We as pastors may indeed be agents of change, at times, when used by God. But this activity will be marked by spiritual discipline and full attention to the more primary pastoral tasks of teaching and modeling the Gospel.

The three words in the AIM model as applied to the Change Agent model are:

A stands for *aware*

I stands for *implant*

M stands for *manage*

Awareness in handling the stress of change agentry includes several factors. First, change agentry is seldom the primary role of the pastor. Second, change agentry is most effective when built upon a solid base of pastoring. Third, the time-honored roles of pastor are faithfully witnessing to the Gospel and ministering to the needs of human beings. Fourth, people don't want to be changed and will resist such efforts—therefore don't be surprised at the backlash. Fifth, only God has the right to change people. If God calls us to this task of bringing change, we must carry out the task with spiritual discipline lest we be meeting only our own ego needs or distortions. Sixth, when God leads and the church rises up to bring change, this is a mighty experience and we should all work for it; but we should not assume we have the right, the wisdom, or the power to make this happen according to our will. And, finally, the kingdom of God has not come yet. It will come and we are called to live faithfully by its tenets, but it will come only in God's time and by God's power.

The two biggest stress factors in change agentry among pastors lie in their physical, emotional, and spiritual limits—human beings cannot long endure the stress of all-out change agentry—and in the distortion of pastoral thinking and the consequent reaction amongst laity when the pastor assumes the change agent role.

The burnout factor in pastoral change agentry has been apparent in many counseling and denominational offices for several years now. This certainly causes us to ask some serious questions about the change agent role. There is no question that God occasionally asks us pastors (and other leaders) to sacrifice our all for a ministry task. Sometimes a whole group or generation of leaders is sacrificed. I believe this happened in the recent racial and anti-war efforts by some clergy. But I see this as an occasional phenomenon, not the primary task of pastoral ministry. If a person feels called by God to be a change agent, he or she may well be right but such a person should give careful thought to whether this should be done through the pastoral role or through another role inside or outside of the institutional church.

The other serious stress factor in change agentry is the distortion in pastoral thinking and the laity's reaction to this. The pastor who feels his/her primary task is to change people or situations is bound to experience serious frustration because few such changes are accomplished easily. But the distortion lies in the feeling of this pastor that the only way she or he can be a success is by changing things and in always looking for things to change. Such a person evaluates his or her ministry in terms of what has been changed. If one can't change big things, one will turn to almost any change simply to prove one's worth as a pastor.

The parishioners of this pastor, of course, sense this drive to change them or their situations. They respond predictably with resistance, violence, or quiet stubbornness, for nobody wants another person to change him or her according to that other person's ideas unless he or she is mentally disordered. Even when the pastor tries to accomplish the changes in a nice way, the people get the message: "I am unacceptable to this pastor, and (s)he will change me or my situation if I don't resist." So instead of meeting people where they are and administering God's forgiveness and love, the change agent concentrates on producing guilt or fear and punishing any refusal to change. Instead of modeling the Gospel and with the apostle Paul pointing to the way of love, ". . . I will show you a still more excellent way" (I Cor. 12:31), she or he forces change according to her or his own idea of what needs to be changed.

The result is predictable—the parishioners resist and fight back, and the pastor feels like a failure and/or exhausts her or his energy in fighting with parishioners. Even parishioners who supported the pastor at first often run out of energy or leave the church in frustration. It is important to note that by accepting people as they are, the pastor does not have to be like them. She or he only gives up the assumed right to change them.

The long tradition of pastoring in the Christian church has been built upon faithful witness to the Gospel and caring for human needs. The change agentry process may well be necessary occasionally, but seldom as the primary role of the pastor.

The "I" word in the model is "implant". This is the role-specific word in the AIM model for handling change agentry. The great model for this is Jesus in his constant teaching and modeling ministry. The apostle Paul is our other model. This role as planter of the seed is clearly stated in 1 Corinthians 3:6.

The idea of planting reminds us that pastors, through their teaching, preaching, and modeling, point out and encourage change-agent work in other lives. The pastor plants the seeds for social justice, sharing, caring, and sacrificial stewardship. These are the beginnings of a salvation with a wider outreach than our own. This role, planter of the seed, is difficult for the impatient and for those not willing to develop the spiritual discipline which undergirds pastoring nor willing to learn the love and patience required in teaching people and ministering to their needs even when not agreeing with their beliefs or life-styles.

The "M" word again is "manage" and again the key is decision making. The decisions in change agentry lie in deciding what the ministry needs are in a given situation, what the best methods of teaching and caring to meet these needs are, and how to keep oneself as a pastor most open and ready for God's leading whether that be the intense effort of being a change agent or the more patient effort of teaching and caring.

Change agents are needed. Perhaps we should designate such an office in the church, but the pastor trying to be a change agent often distorts his or her pastoral vision, confuses parishioners, generates considerable destructive as well as helpful conflict, and, in my judgment, is often not true to the great pastoral roles of the New Testament models.

13
Try Smarter, Not Harder

The myth of intensity has a powerful influence in our society. It says that any task can be accomplished if enough effort is applied, and that the only good people are those who work hard.

This Protestant Work Ethic, as it is often called, is the social religion of our society. Its priests are the workaholics. Its devotees are the guilt-laden masses who believe and struggle with its everyday conflicts. Its pagans are those who do not believe it but must live in a system which honors those who do.

Pastors are particularly vulnerable to this myth for several reasons. First, the church since the Reformation has helped push this work ethic. Second, as the only paid leader in the local church, the pastor is often expected to "make it all happen." And third, two of the professional roles of the pastor are the helper and change agent roles with the goal to bring about results in ministry.

Like all myths, this myth of intensity has some truth in it. Hard work is important in achieving goals much of the time. (There is the danger of laziness when it comes to fulfilling one's potential in God's purposes.) And enthusiasm and hard work do have a powerful unifying effect in bringing the people of God together in common ministry to each other and those outside the church.

Our theological heritage encourages work/action. In the Old Testament God was continually urging the people to action; in the New Testament Jesus was an active preacher, teacher, and healer. And we know that spiritual discipline and action are important to our personal faith as well as to our ministry. Our own heritage and teachings, then, would seem to push us into acting as if the myth of intensity were true.

All around us in our society the approval and rewards go to people who work the hardest, accomplish a great deal, or accumulate more than others. It is interesting to note what our society has done with this semi-religious notion that hard work is the answer to everything. We have made heroes of the athletic competitors who "give 110 percent in every game," the executive who puts in long hours, the "dedicated" teacher, the sacrificial/hardworking wife and mother, the straight-'A' student, etc. Society has taken a good idea and raised it to the level of idolatry.

Are hard work and intense effort all bad? Of course not. The idolatrous dimension of the mythology surrounding hard work makes analysis of it difficult. How can we sort out the myth from reality?

Nearly every day pastors share with me the story of their struggles. Some are trying to change an apathetic church into an evangelizing church. Some are dealing with a clique in the church which demands that things go its way. Some are struggling with a disappointing career. Some are wrestling with marital and family problems. And some are struggling with their own spiritual growth and discipline.

One of the stories I hear most often is from pastors who used to take a day off, who used to take time for devotion and study, who used to have time to listen when people needed to talk to them. They are now slaves to the myth of intensity; yet they barely meet their deadlines, and they come to the end of nearly every day worrying about all the things they should have done.

The solution seems simple enough: Slow down! Don't try to do it all! Relax! (Isn't it an interesting contradiction finding yourself *trying harder to relax!*)

By God's grace we have a formula for handling this struggle. And it is not strange that the formula comes from the mouth of Jesus: "Come unto me, all ye that labor and are heavy laden, and I will give you rest. Take my yoke upon you, and learn of me; for I am meek and lowly in heart: and ye shall find rest unto your souls. For my yoke is easy, and my burden is light" (Matthew 11:28-30, KJV).

I imagine we have all preached on this pericope but what does it mean to a harried pastor in a technological, capitalistic society which believes the myth of intensity? Let us preach it to ourselves by noting the simple guidelines in this text.

First, "Come unto me. . . ." The answer to our struggle is not "out there" nor in more intense worship of the myth. The answer is in God. That seems nice and theological but what does it mean? We don't know what it means until we interrupt the frenzied pursuit of the myth and turn our focus upon God.

Second, "all ye that labor and are heavy laden." You got it, God—that's me. But I'm trying so hard for your sake! All this effort is for that noble calling we name ministry. Or is it?

Third, "I will give you rest." That sounds mighty attractive, God. But what do I do with all my guilt feelings and anxiety about unfinished work if I rest? I guess I really don't dare rest. Sorry about that!

Fourth, "Take my yoke upon you and learn of me." Now, wait a minute, God. I've already got more than I can do. I can't take on another task. I do sometimes wonder though if you aren't offering me a better option.

Fifth, "I am meek and lowly of heart and ye shall find rest unto your souls." But, God, I've tried that meek and lowly route. People walk all over me when I do that. Anyway, this is an age of power—you have to fight for what you want. If I am meek and lowly, the injustices in the world keep piling up. But then, you sure seemed to accomplish some great things through the meek and lowly Jesus. I do remember the rhythm he set up between rest and meditation and dedicated effort.

Sixth, "For my yoke is easy, and my burden is light." O God, I keep getting the feeling that there is a better way of doing ministry than constantly trying harder. You talk about a yoke and a burden and how these are easier than my way. I'd really like to know. What does this mean?

My little homily in personal prayer style is obviously designed to set up an answer. The answer comes from a combination of theology, psychology, and management techniques. Here is how it comes out:

1. Hard work and intense effort have value when they are attached to a clear goal and are supported by the rhythm between work, rest, and self-nurture.
2. God is still in charge. I am not responsible for bringing the kingdom of Heaven to earth all by myself. I am only called to be faithful in proclamation and personal living.
3. If I take time to really see what is going on, I can find more creative ways to handle the tasks of ministry.

4. It is out of this taking time to look at the situation and to think about it and to meditate so that God's spirit may lead me (us) that new possibilities emerge. Then I can try smarter, not harder.

When I keep banging my nose up against the same stone wall, I can continue doing that and get used to the taste of my own blood or I can run away or I can back off and start observing the situation and ask myself sensible questions about the stone wall and my relationship to it. When I choose this last course of action, I will usually be able to figure out a more creative way of handling the stone wall with God's help and a little help from my friends. I will use a lot less energy doing so.

Try smarter, not harder!

14

The Pastor's Support System

In this final chapter I want to discuss the conscious effort by pastors to build a personal support system which undergirds pastoral ministry.

The goal of the pastoral support system is not just to avoid clergy burnout. Its goal is also to enrich pastoral ministry and personal growth by pastors. Of course, we assume that this will result in benefits to the whole church and its ministry.

The pastoral support system may be likened to a three-legged stool. One leg of the stool is the pastor's own self-esteem and self-nurture. The second leg is the pastor's intimate relationships which may include marriage, family, peers, and close friends. The third leg is the pastor's spiritual support and discipline system. Each of these legs on the stool is important, for eliminating one or more of the legs makes the stool, and support system, shaky or ineffective.

The first leg of this support system is the pastor's own self-care process. This may seem self-centered or an indulgence in pampering instead of the disciplined dedication that it is. It turns out, however, that learning to nurture ourselves as pastors accomplishes several important objectives.

First, self-nurture honors our individual responsibility to God for stewardship of ourselves. Each of us is the only person God ever created exactly this way. We each have a unique responsibility to develop this self to its full potential ("talents") as a self and to its fullest potential as a ministering instrument.

As pastors we have a calling to model the difficult combination of self-care and giving ourselves to others. Our contemporary world is full of opportunities to be self-indulgent and self-centered. The world also presents the self-sacrificing, altruistic person as the ideal for humanity. I believe we are learning in this generation that these two models are not the only options. The healthiest option is a middle one: taking time to nurture ourselves but with the goal of nurturing ourselves so as to develop ourselves into instruments of ministry for the glory of God.

This process of self-nurture and developing myself into an instrument of ministry involves my full self—body, mind, and spirit. If I neglect any part, I do not reach my full potential as a whole person. The model of self which is my goal is the biblical model of wholeness and the model of Jesus as a ministering instrument.

Wholeness in the biblical sense is different from the medical model of health, the capitalistic model of accumulation and comfort, the success model of achievement and status, or the psychiatric model of freedom from psychosis and neurosis. Biblical wholeness is a very special understanding of what a human being is. It says that wholeness must be big enough to include our pain and suffering as well as our health and joy. It says wholeness is complete only when all persons are whole: each of us can experience some degree of wholeness, but true wholeness does not occur until it is experienced corporately. Biblical wholeness is not an end in itself. Its function and value lie in using wholeness for the corporate good. We are whole when we are forgiven, loved, and serving God, not just when we feel good and have no problems.

Wholeness in the biblical sense not only includes suffering and pain but also suggests that we learn and grow through failures and hurts. This not only legitimizes these experiences; it also denies the contemporary American dream of full health, wealth, and happiness as the goal of living. This concept of wholeness does not make pain attractive but it helps us accept, understand, and grow by our pain.

The body, mind, and spirit dimensions of self-awareness and self-nurture do not imply a fragmentary self, but these categories may focus our self-care more specifically. Each category is interdependent. We cannot ignore the care of the body and not experience some deficit in the health of the spirit, for example. We need to learn that caring for the body, though, means meeting its basic needs, not indulging all its learned wants.

Bodily nurture involves commonsense nutrition, exercise, change of pace, work, and rest. They are simple ingredients but the temptation and pressure not to take them seriously abounds for pastors. A poorly cared-for body will be a more limited instrument of ministry.

Mental health is almost a cult in our society. The popular notion built upon psychiatric and capitalistic ideas equates mental health with adjustment to society and the ability to consume things happily. As pastors, we can provide the pastoral care-model of the person whose mind is occupied with God's purposes, service to others, and the values of life which take God's creation seriously (Proverbs 4:7, 23: Matthew 6:21; John 7:38; 1 Peter 1:22).

The second leg of the support stool is our intimate relationships. It takes time to build and maintain these intimate relationships. We pastors often feel we already spend enough time with people. Sometimes we feel we don't have enough time for our work, much less just sitting and socializing with family or friends. Such feelings are misleading. We need relationships where we are just persons with the same needs and joys as others. Time spent in such relationships is not wasted or optional. This is valuable time in keeping us human, in keeping us pastors from having a distorted view of ourselves and others. Such time is certainly valuable to those with whom we have intimacy commitments (1 Timothy 3).

Clergy peer-support groups are an especially valuable resource for clergy nurture and support. There are lectionary study groups, contract groups, prayer groups, sensitivity groups, exercise groups, study groups, and so on. The key ingredients seem to be intentionality (all agree to the purposes of the group and attend regularly) and buoyancy (supporting each other so no one sinks under pressure). Our Office of Pastoral Services has helped a number of these groups get started. We find them to be most helpful for pastors as persons and professionals.

The nurture of the spirit completes the wholeness trilogy: body, mind, and spirit. It is the third leg of our support stool.

Nurturing the spirit and developing a spiritual discipline and relationship to God are sometimes neglected by pastors. We may feel we had so much theology in seminary that we don't need to study it seriously now. We may feel that Scripture reading and individual prayer are things to be done only in sermon preparation and for the professional functions. Anyway, the real work of ministry is out there working with people.

Such thoughts may keep us from nurturing ourselves spiritually.

It is not uncommon for me to hear pastors, in my counseling sessions with them, speak of being dried up spiritually or confused and full of spiritual doubts. It's all right to have doubts and have spiritual low times. These can be lessened, however, by spiritual self care. Our pastoral ministry often comes alive when spiritual disciplines are initiated.

The nurturing of the spirit has other dimensions also. Studying and absorbing the fine arts (drama, painting, and music) are most valuable pursuits with which to nurture the spirit. The reading of fine literature and discussing the great thinkers of history expand and nurture the spirit. Spending time with those we love and need, listening, watching, caring, and just being ourselves will nurture the spirit. Traveling and having associations with people outside the church often nurture the spirit. Time in the outdoors, opening the self to the rest of God's creation, nurtures the spirit.

The life of the spirit is not a weird, out-of-touch experience. It is the counter-culture Jesus suggested and modeled; it is a "high" which is not built around TV, consumption, and busyness. But it does not come naturally for most people, including pastors. The life of the spirit is literally an "altered state of consciousness" in our society. We must make decisions, use our will, and set up different habit patterns if we are not to succumb to the cultural religion and the drive to consume, accumulate, and achieve in our society. This all takes a surrender of ourselves to God's purposes, much as Jesus had to surrender and empty himself to become the instrument of God's salvation (Philippians 2:1-11). Pietism and spiritual rituals as such are not the goal. But without spiritual discipline and nurture we will not be spiritual leaders.

Much of the stress we experience as pastors comes from distorted thinking about our pastoral "calling" and from not taking time to nurture body, mind, and spirit. The person with a clear sense of purpose ("calling"), who keeps his or her three-legged support stool solidly in place, can handle a lot of pressure and accomplish a great deal in ministry without burnout.

How long has it been since your dreams, hopes, and spiritual "vision" have turned you on? The joy of ministry and the relaxed confidence in your own worth and future can only be generated within you and by your own decision. It cannot be provided magically or spiritually by someone else or by performing ministry tasks. Therefore, the self-awareness, self-nurture, self-sharing, and decision-making we've discussed in this book depend upon your opening yourself to the creative possibilities God offers.

I pray that the information, the models, and the insights of this book will trigger your own creative effort to become aware of yourself, nurture yourself, and develop yourself for the joy of living, the joy of intimacy, the joy of ministry, to the greater glory of God. Burnout is not the inevitable outcome of dedicated pastoring.

Appendix

The Power
of Invitation

Invitation is a relatively unused way of relating to other persons.
Using the power of invitation requires me to give up the usual
methods of coercion, manipulation, rebellion, accommodation, or
withdrawal. It requires me to think of myself and other persons in
a different way. Coercion and manipulation are my attempts to get
other persons to do what I want or what I think ought to be done.
Withdrawal, accommodation, and rebellion are my attempts to de-
fend myself against the power I feel other persons have over me.

Invitation takes seriously my need to have other persons in my
world and it gives up the belief that I have a right to make other
persons be what I want them to be. Through invitation I not only
take my needs seriously, I also honor the needs of other persons to
be who they are. Therefore, when I invite other persons to share an
experience or material things or a lifetime with me, I invite them *as
they are* to share with me *as I am.* I hope then that they will accept
my invitation and similarly invite me to share something with them.
But since true invitation does not guarantee that the other person
will accept or that I will get what I want, I must be prepared to take
responsibility for my own needs and to relate to others without
blaming, forcing, or manipulating them.

Obviously, invitation is not as effective as power plays in controlling
other persons or in getting what I want, but it opens up the possibility
for human beings to relate to each other without the power plays
we usually use. Jesus is a remarkable example of relating to other
persons through invitation. Over and over he modeled God's will for

us and invited people to join him in living it. Some tried; many refused. God relates to us through invitation and therefore urges us to relate to each other in this way.

The following diagram shows three agendas for human behavior most of us experience. Being aware of these agendas helps us understand our behavior and that of others. Knowing these agendas will help us understand why invitation is often difficult.

Read over the agenda chart. Then think over the questions below so you can experiment more effectively with using invitations in your relationships to others, and so you can better understand their invitations to you.

1. List some of the important invitations in your past, which you have given or responded to.
2. What invitations in your past have given you the most trouble?
3. What invitations in your past have you handled well?
4. What are the key ingredients of these invitations which help them to be handled well or poorly?
5. What invitations are unresolved in your marriage, family, work, school, or friendships right now?
6. How do you think you could give and receive invitations more effectively?
7. How do you think each of the agendas on the chart affects invitations between persons?

Agendas for Human Behavior

People are often unable to communicate/cooperate because they are on different behavior agendas. Each agenda has its own characteristics. To facilitate communication/cooperation, a leader must recognize and satisfy the often hidden agenda.

AGENDA	EMOTION	BEHAVIOR
RELATIONSHIP (integrate thinking and feeling)	Joy (positive) / Sadness (negative)	There is concern for others. Dialogue and cooperation are important. There is a modesty of individual behavior. Listening is important. Spontaneous behavior and creative ideas are frequent. Body language is relaxed and animated. The key issue is to achieve the maximum benefit for all. Easily frustrated by hypocrisy and divisiveness.
IDENTITY (thinking more dominant)	Love (positive) / Anger (negative)	The major issues here are, "Who am I?" and "What's in it for me?" Behavior is attention-seeking and approval-seeking. Anger occurs when the persons are resisted or put down. Role playing is frequent and body language is distinctive or anxious. Positively, people on this agenda like causes and responsibility. They seek assurance that they are worthwhile.
SURVIVAL (feelings more dominant)	Pleasure (positive) / Fear (negative)	The "law of the jungle" prevails, even if in a sophisticated manner. Persons on this agenda are stubborn, fearful, resist change. Their body language is often belligerent or defensive. The only message they can really hear is assurance of survival. Then they may move to a higher agenda. Positively, they make powerful allies and loyalists.

Growth in openness and relating →

Pressure of Events and Feelings →

It is important to note that, given pressure or difficult decisions, most people will revert to the next lower agenda. Enough pressure forces all people to the survival agenda. Good results in a meeting or activity can occur in all agendas, but maximum benefit comes when everyone is on the relationship agenda. This is also the most tenuous agenda. A perceptive leader can read his own and others' agendas and fit the meeting or activity process to the indicated agendas.

Notes

Chapter 2

[1]G. Lloyd Rediger, "Let's Get the Pastor," *The Christian Ministry,* vol. 9, no. 2 (March, 1978), pp. 30-32.

[2]G. Lloyd Rediger, "The Change Agent Model: Some Practical Considerations," *The Christian Ministry,* vol. 5, no. 1 (January, 1974), pp. 32-33.

[3]G. Lloyd Rediger, "The Myth of Intensity," unpublished paper.

[4]Hans Selye, *Stress Without Distress* (New York: New American Library, Inc., Signet Books, 1974), p. 27.

[5]A. R. Wyler, M. Masuda, and Thomas H. Holmes, "Magnitude of Life Events and Seriousness of Illness," *Psychosomatic Medicine,* vol. 33 (March-April, 1971), pp. 115-122.

[6]Abraham H. Maslow, *Toward a Psychology of Being* (Princeton, N.J.: D. Van Nostrand Co. division of Litton Educational Publishing, Inc. 1962).

[7]The Office of Pastoral Services is a program of the Wisconsin Conference of Churches. It is a confidential and ecumenical counseling service for clergy and their immediate families only. It has counseling stations in Milwaukee, Appleton, and Eau Claire. Madison is the home office. G. Lloyd Rediger is the director.

[8]The Wisconsin Conference of Churches' statistics, compiled in the 1980 Wisconsin Religious Directory, list a total clergy population of 7,513.

Chapter 3

[1]Viktor E. Frankl, *Man's Search for Meaning: An Introduction to Logo-therapy,* trans. Ilse Lasch, (Boston: Beacon Press, 1959).

[2]Abraham H. Maslow, *Toward a Psychology of Being* (Princeton, N.J.: D. Van Nostrand Co. division of Litton Educational Publishing, Inc. 1962).

Chapter 5

[1]Margaretta K. Bowers, *Conflicts of the Clergy* (New York: Thomas Nelson, Inc., 1963) p. 35 ff.

[2]James E. Dittes, "Psychological Characteristics of Religious Professionals" in *Research on Religious Development,* ed. Merton P. Strominen (New York: Hawthorn Books, Inc., 1971) p. 429 ff.

[3]James E. Dittes, *Ministers on the Spot* (Philadelphia: The Pilgrim Press, 1970), especially pp. 16-22.

[4]Samuel Blizzard, "The Minister's Dilemma," *The Christian Century*, vol. 73, no. 3 (March, 1956), pp. 508-510.

[5]Jeffrey K. Hadden, *The Gathering Storm in the Churches* (Garden City, N.Y.: Doubleday & Co. Inc., 1969), pp. 211-235, 241.

[6]John E. Biersdorf, "The Crisis in the Ministry," North American ed. (New York: IDOC/International, 1971).

[7]Gerald Jud, et al., *Ex-Pastors: Why Men Leave the Parish Ministry* (Philadelphia: Pilgrim Press, United Church Press, 1970).

[8]Edgar W. Mills and John P. Koval, "Stress in the Ministry," North American ed. (New York: IDOC/National, 1971).

[9]Edgar W. Mills, "Types of Role Conflict Among Clergymen," *Ministry Studies*, vol. 2, nos. 3, 4 (1968).

[10]My article, "The Feminine Mystique and the Ministry," *The Christian Century*, vol. 96, no. 23 (July 4-11, 1979), pp. 699-702, gives a summary of the early experience we had counseling women pastors. Subsequent experience shows women essentially normalizing their role in the same way men do, although some women continue to seek to make a unique gender-oriented contribution to ordained ministry.

Chapter 7

[1]John E. Biersdorf, ed., *Creating an Intentional Ministry* (Nashville: Abingdon Press, 1976).

[2]C. West Churchman, *The Systems Approach* (New York: Delacorte Press/division of Dell Publishing Co., Inc., 1968).

[3]Irving L. Janis, "Groupthink," *Psychology Today* (November, 1971), pp. 43-46, 74-76.

[4]Peter F. Drucker points out the value in this process in his book *Management: Tasks, Responsibilities, Practices* (New York: Harper & Row, Publishers, Inc., 1974), pp. 466-470.

Chapter 9

[1]This subject is covered well in the book, *How Do I Say I Love You*, written by William J. Krutza, (Grand Rapids: Baker Book House, 1980).

Chapter 10

[1]James M. Gustafson, *Treasure in Earthen Vessels* (New York: Harper & Row, Publishers, Inc., 1961).